Self esteem in the classroom
techniques for teachers

Lila Swell, Ed. D.
Queens College,
City University of New York

KENDALL/HUNT PUBLISHING COMPANY
4050 Westmark Drive   Dubuque, Iowa 52002

Contents

ACKNOWLEDGMENT

This book was written at the request of many students and teachers who attended "Educating For Success" seminars throughout the country. They were in need of specific classroom techniques with which to apply the principles of EFS to their own students. Many of the ideas contained in this book resulted from the experiences and thinking of these teachers and students. It would be impossible to name each of them individually. However, I hope that this acknowledgment conveys my deepest appreciation for their encouragement and contributions.

I would like to dedicate this book to all the children whose best selves I hope will emerge.

To the teachers who will use this book I have this to say. The greatest gift you can give your students is your understanding, appreciation and respect for their individual identities. It is the deepest responsibility of educators to help students to develop as individuals so that they will become their own best selves.

CHAPTER ONE

Introduction to humanistic education

Who am I? Where am I going? What am I doing? These are questions which are asked frequently by people of all ages, and in all walks of life in our Twentieth Century world.

The world we live in is fraught with change as no other period in the history of humanity has been before. These changes include the replacement of people by machines, eliminating jobs which were considered staples of the workplace. The global economy has imposed the need for relocation in order to be on top of things in faraway places. Relocations are disruptive. Political upheavals — some for better and some for worse — are becoming more common all the time. What was once considered sophisticated weaponry turns out to be easily reproduced by relatively unsophisticated science students, and thus, can be easily acquired by groups with less than desirable qualities — like fanatics.

By no means, are all the changes bad. Medicine, science, psychology, the arts as well as many other fields, have taken giant steps to alleviate the individual's pain and suffering and to increase their pleasure. However, social indices of discontent seem to be on the rise — the divorce rate, substance abuse, dropout rates, homelessness, and on and on.

Coping with the stresses of life is a difficult task for adults. Imagine what it is like for children.

Children, usually are not members of sensitivity groups, and rarely do they seek the umbrella of a new (or old) religion to solve their problems. In fact, children look to their parents for solutions to their problems — and to their teachers. Problems of the "new math" or "adolescent complexion" genre can be solved by cadres of analysts drawn from sources as diverse as teachers and classmates. When the problems are more intimate, when they involve searching for self, who can help? Their parents are seeking the answers to the same questions of self-identity, self-confidence, self-doubt. Without some modification it seems that society is doomed to continuously regenerate emotionally barren citizens, incapable of relating to others because they do not know how to relate to themselves. Problems which may not be able to be solved in the home, but which must be solved to insure a continuous and healthy society, are going to have to be solved in the classroom.

We have already seen some of our most devoutly held educational principles shattered by the same technology that replaced man by a machine. There is no longer 100 percent assurance that teaching a skill to train someone to perform a job-related task is essential to a curriculum because tomorrow that job may not exist. The necessity for humanity to survive and, to interrelate with other human beings, will never cease to exist — that's indisputable.

Why then are curriculums centered on subject matter still being pushed by our most prominent educators as the be-all and end-all of education to the exclusion of the development of the self? "Humanistic education" is the beginning of what has got to be the most important trend in modern education. It would be foolish to say that the traditional subjects of reading, writing and 'rithmetic should be eliminated from the classroom. No one has suggested that, but if education is indeed a preparation for life then it would be a serious crime of omission to neglect the self as a subject to be taught. Individualization of children, and helping them very early on to see their strengths, builds the self and enhances the learning process. Gearing the curriculum to encompass the child's interests and using innate strengths to build a positive repertoire of successes can do nothing less than transform a potential truant into an honor student. One may look at life as a continuum of micro lives — pre-school, school, advanced school, career, job, marriage, etc. One's performance in each micro-life usually portends the future of the next; that is, successful experiences seem to occur in higher and higher ratios as one progresses from step to step. The implication is no tautology; indeed, success breeds success.

We know that in order to learn, children must have a positive view of themselves, to see themselves as adequate and worthy. If we stereotype them or have one measure or standard of successful functioning into which the children do not fit, then we have failed them as educators, for we have taken away their most precious possession, their identity and uniqueness. We must not only believe, but also cherish, the notion that people are different and they have a right to that differentness. So the questions arise: How can we as teachers bring to birth that unique potential in our children? What tools can we give them to deal with life? Our society is changing so rapidly that educators must prepare children to use their strengths in a variety of ways. But if our curriculum is focused on the inculcation of skills for occupations which may disappear and there is no corresponding focus on the development of the student's self-image, how can individuals adapt to the changing roles they may need to play in the shifting structure of society?

The development of the unique capacities of each student should be the fulcrum of our curriculum. Learning is risking into unknown territory, and the child needs to develop confidence within a supportive environment. This is the function of the educator, to nourish and care for students as one would a garden. One does not grow in an environment fraught with fear, anxiety, mistrust and criticism. One grows with love, kindness, nourishment, and care. Some people believe that the only way one learns is through fear, punishment, and ridicule. They also believe that pointing out failures to people is beneficial to them and will make them learn. A student once told me that her third-grade teacher hung all the flunking papers in front of the room for all the class to see. That teacher must have believed that the child would be frightened into learning and doing better on the next test; that she would develop courage because failure builds character. From everything we know of learning, this is ludicrous. People are debilitated and weakened by failure. True, a negative experience may sometimes be growth-producing, but only after one has built up a reservoir of successes. Suppose you just learned how to drive a car and every time you drove you had an accident. Would you drive again?

A personal feeling of adequacy is a learned feeling, it comes from successful experiences. A series of successes is not a random occurrence, it is the result of choices carefully made for success and against failure. People who choose success are called smart. It's kind of circular. Success breeds smartness; smartness implies choosing and mastering experiences successfully — which generates more successes and makes one smarter....This is the old self-fulfilling prophecy. People feel adequate through mastery of things they accomplish and positive success experiences — not failures.

This book is about enhancing the self. It is not a general science or algebra or American history text, but is meant to be used in conjunction with texts for all courses. Each of the following chapters begins with a brief introduction which is followed by a series of techniques specifically designed for use by teachers, grades kindergarten through high school. The techniques, which can be incorporated into the existing curriculum, are designed to highlight and reinforce the individual student's successes, strengths, values and methods of handling conflict. In short, they:

1. help students become aware of themselves;
2. help students become aware of each other;
3. help further the teachers' understanding of the students;
4. help both teachers and students actualize their awareness.

The techniques are divided into those applicable to the early childhood and elementary levels and those best used in junior and senior high school. This is not to say, however, that each technique can be used only in the grade or subject specified. The categories are meant only as a guide; for with ingenuity the techniques can easily be adapted to other grade levels.

Chapter Two, "Appreciating Success," is grounded in the theory that success breeds success. Because acknowledging one's successes as well as one's special talents is a giant step along the road to a positive self-image, the techniques in this chapter are to help children perceive, understand, accept and display their own successes as well as those of their classmates.

Chapter Three, "Tapping and Actualizing Students' Strengths," suggests techniques that will help students to become aware of their own, as well as others, particular strengths. As they actualize their own potential they will become aware of their uniqueness and so further enhance their self-image.

"Values Instruction," Chapter Four, is designed to help students identify, understand and accept their own values, for by so doing they can better choose among alternatives and set and attain more realistic goals.

The two skills needed for management of conflict, both in and out of the classroom, are those of problem-solving and communication. Chapter Five, "Conflict Management," aims at helping students to become aware of and to communicate their own feelings, as well as to understand others' viewpoints. A four-step method which allows for more flexibility in problem-solving is stressed.

CHAPTER TWO

Appreciating success

A positive self-concept is essential for learning in the classroom. The children's own image of themselves should be seen as worthy, adequate, and strong. This image is affirmed by the outside world via approval of themselves and their accomplishments. Their early experiences of success help them to take risks which lead to further success — success breeds success.

Successful experiences help to define, build, and motivate children. They help them to strive harder, to learn better, and to look at learning as an adventure and not something to be feared.

The successes of the children should be identified and labeled by the teacher and displayed to others so that we can recondition children into displaying rather than hiding their successes. Labeling in fact produces behavior that corresponds to the label; for example, if a teacher continually calls a student stupid, he/she most often becomes the class dunce. People assume the characteristics and behavior of the label and fulfill the expectation of the labeler. Why not choose positive attributes as public labels? For example, instead of labeling someone dumb, pick a positive attribute to mention.

Too often, there is a tendency to discount "humble" talents. "Yes, I type exceptionally well — but that's not important." "Sure, I guess I do know a lot about art — but that's just a hobby — it doesn't really count." Such depreciation of talents may at first glance seem a virtue, humility. However, there is a world of difference between the insecure person who must continually impress others by boasting, and another person with a realistic appraisal of his/her strengths as well as his/her short-comings.

Our society has discouraged people from displaying their talents — has put negative labels on this act by calling it bragging or exhibitionism. The purpose of the following exercises are to do just the opposite — that is to help children exhibit their own successes and perceive the successes of other children in the classroom.

Early Childhood/Elementary School

1. Identifying success in classmates

Procedures:

1. Write the names of the children in the classroom on the blackboard in alphabetical order.
2. Pass out large rectangular sheets of paper.
3. Have children fold them in half, then fold one side of the half again making three columns.
4. In the first column, have the children copy the children's names.
5. In the second column, have the children write what they think is outstanding about the child.
6. In the third column, have the children explain why they selected the quality they wrote in column two.
7. After the children complete the three columns for everyone in the class (including themselves), have them come one by one to the head of the class and read their remarks into a tape recorder.
8. Take pictures of their responses
9. Record how they felt when they heard what the other children thought of them.
10. Place pictures on the bulletin board with the caption "happiness is . . . . "
11. Have the children complete the statement and this too is displayed for all to see.

Materials:

Large rectangular pieces of paper, markers, tape recorder.

2. Success, American style

Procedures:

1. Have children think about a time when they felt successful.
2. Have children write a small vignette about their successes.
3. Have children share their successes.

   See the following Success Evaluation chart.

Success Evaluation Chart

(This chart was constructed by a group of participants age 8.)

Peter	artist	Because he always draws or has great ideas for decorating our classroom. We needed rockets, he made them.
Elaine	running	Because she always wins running games during lunch time. We were playing tag and she never got caught.
Philip	friendly	Because he's always friendly to other people. He's always kind to everyone in the school yard.
Michael	joking	Because he's always funny and can take a joke. We were playing a trick on him in the school yard, and he didn't get mad.
Terence	baseball	Because he's always hitting home-runs. We were playing a game and we were behind, but he made a hit.
Michael	running	Because we all run after him and can never catch him.

Ann	helping	Because she always helps her sister. We were cleaning and she helped a lot.
Steven	sketching	Because he is always sketching. He sketched a picture of a boat and did good.
Ann Marie	thoughtful	Because she is always willing to help. She helped her sister with a play we were doing.
Christine	kind	Because she would play with everyone. She played with five kids instead of one.
Robert	spelling	Because he always gets 100% and gets words right when they are asked of him.
Jean	willing	Because she was crippled but always would try to play. She would try to play jump rope or something.
Brian	clowning	Because he can always make people laugh.

3. Success newspaper

Procedures:

1. Have the children in class publish a monthly "Success Newspaper".
2. Have the children take turns writing about the goals they or others in the group have achieved.
3. Have children share individual and group successes.

4. Magic wand

Procedures:

1. Make a magic wand.
2. Explain to the children that when you tap them on the head they can become any person they want.
3. Have children play the role of this special person, allowing them to express the qualities that they think are successful.

Materials:

"Magic Wand"

5. Display areas

Procedure:

For each curriculum area, provide a place where children can display the projects they've worked on - Science table, art corner, etc.

6. Mock elections

Procedures:

1. Ask children to pretend that they are running for class President.
2. Have children explain a past deed that they would base their campaign on.
3. Have children present their campaign speech to the class.

7. Relating to famous people

Procedures:

1. Bring pictures of famous people from various ethnic groups that represent the class.
2. Enhance children's self-concept by showing them pictures of famous people from their ethnic groups and what they have accomplished.

Materials:

Pictures of famous people from various ethnic groups.

8. Role-playing with puppets

Procedures:

Provide puppets for role-playing. Have the children act out things that are important to them. They will gain a sense of importance and confidence as others listen to them. Puppets are particularly useful in making shy children feel more comfortable. They allow children to speak up while they are hidden behind the face of something else. Props and costumes can also be used for role-playing — you can provide items or let the children use their imaginations and create their own props.

Materials:

Puppets

9. Doctor, lawyer, Indian chief

Procedures:

1. Have the children draw pictures of the "uniform" they will be wearing when they grow up.
2. Collect all the pictures and have the children guess which picture belongs to each child.
3. Discuss why.

Materials:

Colored marking pens, paper

10. Pictures of story characters

Procedures:

1. Ask each child to relate a story for the class dealing with a specific type of character that he/she likes.
2. Have children explain why they like that particular character.
3. Have the class paint or draw pictures of what they think the character looks like.

Materials:

Paint, markers, paper

11. Who am I?

Procedures:

1. Have each student write a composition on "Who Am I?"
2. Read the paragraph aloud and have the class guess who the writer is.
3. Have the writer relate to the class why he/she picked that student.

12. Topics for short essays

Procedures:

1. Assign short essays on "I Saved the Day When", "My Best Day ", "My Happiest Moment ", "Who Am I?" and/or "Why I like My Friends."
2. Have children share their essays orally in class.

13. Unfinished story

Procedures:

Present the class with an unfinished story about a person who is at the crossroads of his/her life and who must make a decision about a course of action to follow. Have each student finish the story by having the main character choose the most successful course of action (according to the student's own view of success).

14. "I do" carnival

Procedures:

Each child makes an "I Do" button and wears it during the carnival. The children decorate the room in their own way — with signs, paintings, drawings, mobiles, dioramas, sculptures.

Each child has a booth, made by rearranging desks and chairs into individual areas. Within their area children demonstrate what they do that is special — what makes them unique. Children are responsible for their own area, i.e., planning, decorating, activity, and cleaning up. The activity that makes each child special and unique can be class-related or separate from school. The children in the class are free to walk from booth to booth, asking each demonstrator questions regarding their activity or participating in the demonstrator's game. If possible, another class can join the carnival as an audience. Pictures will be taken throughout the carnival, so that the children will see themselves actively engaged in preparation, the end result (the carnival), and, finally, cleaning up.

15. Favorite class activity

Procedures:

> Ask children to paint a picture of what they like to do in class, and then to display the picture and explain why they like that activity.

Materials:

> Paint, canvas/paper

16. Circle discussions

Procedures:

> Children sit in a circle and share their successful experiences. The teacher can start the discussion by asking leading, open ended questions: What happy experiences do you remember that happened to you last week? Last summer? At home? etc. What kinds of things happened that made you feel good about yourself? What do you like about yourself? Why do you like it?

17. Success story speaker

Procedures:

> Every week invite a grown up into the classroom to tell the students about something successful they feel they did at their age. Then discuss the success story with the class. Help them to realize that different people have different measures of success.

18. Success trophy

Procedures:

1. Have each student make a trophy out of the bottom of soda bottles (as the base) and clay (as the figure on top). Brainstorm for titles of achievements and awards, academic as well as social. Some examples could be; Math Wiz, Historian, Best Artist, Class Clown, Neatest Desk, Punctuality Prince/Princess...
2. Take a silent vote for each award. Calculate the winners. Make sure everyone gets at least one award.
3. Engrave each person's name on the correct trophy and distribute them at the final class party. This will become a cherished reminder of their own strengths and successes.

Materials:

Soda bottles, clay

19. Sharing day

Procedures:

1. Children bring an adult to visit the class to see what they have done. Children will have examples of their best work on their desk so they can show off their accomplishments.
2. After showing off their work, the class will put on a little program for the audience. Every child will contribute something: recite a poem, sing, play rhythm band instruments, etc. Then, everyone takes a bow!

Materials:

Things that the children have finished and accomplished in class: coloring books, arithmetic assignments, alphabet charts, etc.

20. Our garden of learning

Procedures:

1. From construction paper cut flowers in the form of daisies in various colors. The center of each flower will have a child's name.
2. Each successful learning experience in class will be recorded on a petal of the child's own personal daisy.

Materials:

Large bulletin board, large colorful construction paper flowers with several petals for each child.

21. End of the week rap

Procedures:

The purpose of this exercise is to foster group spirit and cohesiveness, and to acknowledge individual and class accomplishments.

During the last period of each Friday afternoon, make it a special time for sharing "Good Things" that have happened during the week. These can be either school or personal related things. For instance, if students did well on a test they should tell the others their success. Or, if someone's brother just got married they could share this. Any good event or personal success are the things to be encouraged to share with their fellow students. At first it might seem a little awkward, but after a while the process catches on. A weekly routine is established and the children will all look forward to this special time. Teachers should also be sure to voice their weekly "good happenings" too.

22. Pictures of happiness

Procedures:

1. Have children cut out pictures representing their idea of happiness.
2. Arrange the pictures on oak tag in order to form a picture of something that makes them happy.

Materials:

Magazines, newspapers, scissors, glue, oak tag

23. Happy experiences

Procedures:

1. Children tell about a very happy experience.
2. They may bring in photos to help illustrate the experience.

24. Fishing game

Procedures:

1. Put a paper clip on the end of each fish.
2. Spread them out on a large piece of paper (oak tag) made up to look like water.
3. Construct a fishing pole and line with a magnet on the end of it.
4. Have each fish covered with a picture of a particular job — policeman, fireman, doctor, teacher, etc..
5. Children are not told what to "catch". They must, however, tell why they picked the "caught" fish. i.e., what they liked most about it.

Materials:

Cardboard fish, paper clips, large sheet of oak tag, string and stick for fishing pole, magnet.

25. Class introductions

Procedures:

When meeting the class for the first time, introduce yourself, give background (why I like to teach, etc.). Then
have students write an introduction of themselves, answering such questions as:

- which activities in and outside of school do you enjoy
  most and why?
- what subjects do you enjoy most or are you good at
  and why?
- what do you like about a specific class subject? This
  will get the student to think positively about courses,
  something many of them rarely do.

26. Show and tell

Procedures:

1. Ask the children to bring in something that they feel represents them. Let the children bring in items of
   importance.
2. Have them take turns showing and telling about their
   item to the class.
3. This activity also helps the teacher find out more about
   the individuals in the class

27. Class bulletin board

A bulletin board will be used to display strengths and
achievements of the class. At first, a class slogan must
be decided. (Ex. Fork Lane School fourth graders— "
Fork's Fab Fours") The slogan is to be displayed in the
middle of the board. Students are then asked to write
their names and make a contribution of a personal success they have achieved. (This may be academic if they

choose.) Then as the class achieves successes as a whole, they will be added to their success board. (Ex. perfect attendance for a week, everyone passed a math test, class won sport activity in gym, etc.)

The purpose of this activity is to have students take pride in both their personal and group successes. They will become more aware of their own successes as well as their classmates.

Materials:

bulletin board, magazines, magic markers, superior academic work (individually rated)

28. Footprints of Success

Procedures:

The slogan "Success is one step at a time." will be displayed underneath the bulletin board . Starting at the center of the bulletin board will be footprints. On each footprint will be a success that a student has accomplished.

Example: Bill learned his five times tables.
Joey learned to walk properly in the halls.
Mary learned to raise her hand before speaking.

Footprints can continue off the bulletin board and around the room.

Materials:

Bulletin board, board letters, construction paper, magic marker

29. Keywords of success

Procedures:

1. Teacher holds up word cards constructed out of oak tag. These word cards have "key" words written on them. Each key word is a category.
2. The children in turn, are to tell and/or write the three experiences that they have had in each category which were a success to them.
   Note: In the lesson the teacher can select any category. Some examples of Keywords/Categories are
   SCHOOL, FRIENDS, CAMP, SPORTS
3. Children split up into groups. Each child's success chart is comprised of three experiences in each category, and the reasons why the experience was a success.
4. Each Child is now instructed to write their own definition of Success. "Success to me is when"...
5. Each of the child's category, experience, and why the experience was a success is transposed and written on the strips of oak tag by the children. Like this...

SUCCESS CHART

Category		Experience		Why it was a success
School	1.	In assembly programs, and school plays, I was given a lot of leading roles which were viewed by a large audience.	1.	My teacher, along with my parents, who came to see the school plays discovered I have a lot of acting ability. They encouraged me to take acting lessons. In which case I may make acting my career.
Friends	1. 2. 3.		1. 2. 3.	
Camp	1. 2. 3.		1. 2. 3.	
Sports	1. 2. 3.		1. 2. 3.	

30. Life-size image collage

Procedures:

1. Divide class into small groups.
2. Place wrapping paper the length of child on the floor. A child lies down on the paper, and the group traces his/her form on the paper.
3. Children take turns until each child has had his/her own form outlined on paper.
4. Using the magazine and newspapers, children look for examples or descriptions of their own personality traits such as words, colors, pictures of things they like, etc. Entire figure is to be filled in creating collage.
5. Cut out completed figure to display in class.

Materials:

Brown wrapping paper or butcher paper for each student. Supply of magazines, newspapers, black crayons, glue, scissors.

31. Success mail box

Procedures:

1. Set up a post office with a mail box in the classroom.
2. Each week the student will select a new postmaster.
3. The post office will contain mail slots where each student can receive letters.
4. The beginning of each week, each child will pick a fellow student's name out of a fishbowl.
5. On Friday, students will write a letter/note to their person telling them about what successes/strengths they observed during the week. The completed letter will be placed in the mailbox.

Materials:

Wood, paper, pen, pencils, envelopes, paint, boxes, etc.

32. Television Reviews

Procedures:

Students write and/or illustrate stories about their favorite
TV programs which will reveal their interests.

Materials:

Drawing paper, pens/pencils

Junior High/High School

33. Setting up shop

Procedures:

1. Divide the class into groups of about five students. The groups will work together as a company.
2. Each group will be given a budget in which they will manufacture a new product. It is up to the groups to assign jobs and take on the responsibilities in the company.
3. The company and product will be named and a plan will be designed to sell the product. The groups will decide on the jobs that will need to be filled in order to produce the product.
4. Each person will research and take on the responsibilities of his or her job.
5. The outcome will be a step by step plan on how the company plans to make and sell the product, while staying within the budget.
6. This activity gives students a chance to look at their successes and to use their strengths in order to make the company and the product a success. While working side by side, they will have the opportunity to observe the strengths of their fellow classmates.

34. Pictograms of success

Procedures:

Explain to the class the idea of using codes and ciphers to communicate with one another. In the past the Egyptian written language was hieroglyphics, and today, the Japanese and Chinese use symbols to express themselves. Have each child create a dictionary of pictograms in a notebook. Have children make a list of five successes they have experienced in their life. Translate these successes into pictograms with English translations on the back. Bind them into a success book that may be added to in the future. Keep them in a special place, accessible to all the class. Students will try to decipher each others successes.

35. The recall exercise

Procedures:

This exercise is designed to enable a student to recall and re-experience those moments in their lives when they were accomplishing something.

Tell the students that today we will be playing a memory game. The object of the game is to see how well you can recall the moments and to try to reexperience that moment. Give each of the following directives, one at a time at spaced intervals.

1. Recall a time when you did something well.
2. Recall a time when you felt proud of yourself.
3. Recall a time when you helped someone.
4. Recall a time when you won at a game.
5. Recall a time when you were complimented by your teacher.
6. Recall a time when you felt happy.

Note: Allow your students to actually recreate these past experiences through visual imagery. While they are recalling, they should be silent. At the end of an appropriate interval, ask for their reactions to this "game". As a follow-up to this, you can have the children write about the memory that they most enjoyed recalling.

36. Share a family success

Procedure:

Each student is given an opportunity to tell the class accomplishments that members of their families have achieved. Ensure that it is conducted in a manner which allows students to share, not compete with each other. Encourage students to bring in picture, objects, artifacts, etc., to "illustrate" the achievements they are discussing.

Materials:

Pictures, objects/artifacts to illustrate the achievements

37. "The expert speaks"

Procedures:

Encourage individuals to learn as much as they can in one or two areas that interest them. Then arrange for a series of presentations called "The Expert Speaks".

38. Successful jobs

Procedures:

In an economics course, students can be asked to illustrate how a job they may want to hold someday fits into the national economic system in terms of production, wage earning, spending, contributing goods and services, etc. They should be asked to pick a job that they consider successful. This should provide ample opportunity for an analysis of course material and a chance to see what the students consider successes.

39. Successful people in history

Procedures:

Ask students to choose the person connected with an area of history being studied whom they most admire as a success. Patterns of success can then be established for each student and the history course material will be covered at the same time.

40. Societal definitions of success

Procedures:

When studying the accomplishments of societies and individuals, either past or present, a class could draw conclusions about the varying definitions of success around the world and across time. For example, certain Indian tribes would not consider a deed accomplished at the expense of another person a success. The class could then develop their own definitions of success from their personal experiences.

41. Identifying with music

Procedure:

For a music class, ask children to bring in a record describing their own personality — they may identify with tempo, words, or rhythm. Ask the class if anyone else identifies with the music, and why.

42. Home economics classes

Procedures:

Home economics teachers can develop feelings of success in students using the clothing construction and food preparation segments of the curriculum. Presentation of finished products will reinforce these feelings.

Clothing Construction:

Discuss and display various styles.

Have students choose a pattern according to their own taste.

Make the choices simple so that students can succeed in constructing the garment.

Students can wear the finished garment so that others may admire it and compliment the maker.

Try to encourage students to make more difficult patterns.

Let them develop their own personalities by encouraging their own designs.

Success in construction will develop confidence in their own ability.

Foods:

Discuss different foods according to ingredients, ethnic background, region of origin, family preferences.

Develop a pride in the student's choices, preferences, differences, etc.

Choose foods that are easily prepared and will be successfully prepared.

Encourage experimentation with more difficult preparations.

43. "Symbol of success"

Procedures:

Ask art students to create a symbol of what success means to them. They can use their "Symbol of Success" on all of their work. Their success symbol may be created through a stamp, collage, etc.

Materials:

Linoleum stamp, magazines, glue, paper, markers.

44. Graphing a successful person

Procedures:

In a math class, graph paper is distributed. Ask the students to draw a picture of a person they feel is successful (e.g., Abraham Lincoln) or a hobby they have mastered (e.g., a bowling pin for bowling). If the students have any difficulty in drawing these sketches, they may trace them from other sources. The students are to record the key coordinates of the figure they have drawn and state why they feel the person or hobby is successful. (The coordinates for Abraham Lincoln and Snoopy are given here as examples. These are common figures that might represent success to students.) The teacher can initiate a discussion in which students can compare their own traits and successes with those of their admired successful person. Students may exchange coordinate points with their neighbors, so that they will be given the opportunity to graph another successful figure. Their classmates should give hints to help identify why that person or hobby represents success. This technique will give the students practice in graphing as well as promoting feelings of success.

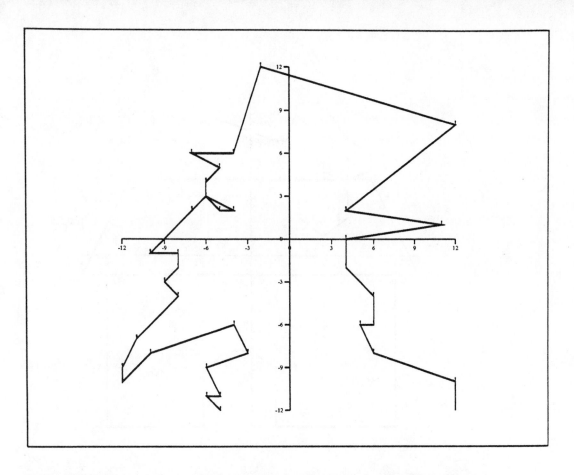

Hints: This person overcame obstacles of poverty and opposition. He was a leader and fought for justice. (-5,-12), (-6,-11), (-5,-11), (-6,-9), (-3,-8), (-4,-6), (-10,-8), (-12,-10), (-12,-9), (-11,-7), (-8,-4), (-9,-3), (-8,-2), (-8,-1), (-10,-1), (-7,2), (-6,3), (-5,2), (-4,2), (-6,3), (-6,4), (-5,5), (-7,6), (-4,6), (-2,12), (12,8), (4,2), (11,1), (4,0), (4,-2), (6,-4), (6,-6), (5,-6), (6,-8), (12,-10), (12,-12).

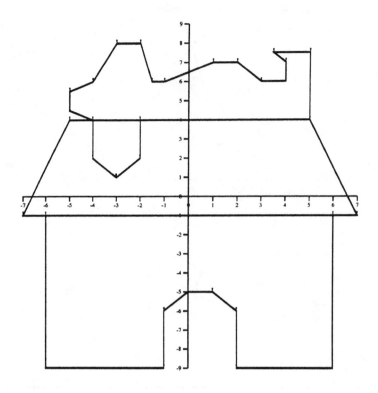

Hints: This character likes people, is innocent and idealistic, and is loved by everyone. (-6,-1), (-6,-9), (-1,-9), (-1,-6), (0,-5), (1,-5), (2,-6), (2,-9), (6,-9), (6,-1), (7,-1), (5,4), (-2,4), (-2,2), (-3,1), (-4,2), (-4,4), (-5, 4.5), (-5, 5.5), (-4,6), (-3,8), (-2,8), (-1.5,6), (-1,6), (1,7), (2,7), (3,6), (4,6), (4,7), (3.5,7.5), (5,7.5), (5,4), (-5,4), (-7,-1), (-6,-1), (6,-1)

45. Venn diagrams

Procedures:

Ask students to represent their successes for different time periods of their life by means of Venn diagrams. Their successes are drawn as sets. They are asked to determine whether any of these successes intersect and whether they are disjoint, and to find the union of these successes by using the mathematical formulas.

46. Number line

Procedures:

Draw a line and number the endpoints -100 and +100. Ask the class to evaluate their personal successes by assigning each success a numeric value within these limits. Then label the points by writing the success at the point on the line corresponding to the numeric value. The student should also use concrete evidence to explain how the score was determined.

Materials:

Graph paper, pencils, rulers.

47. Class, teacher and self evaluations

Procedures:

Provide periodic opportunities for individual student conferences to evaluate the class, teacher, and the student. Do they feel they have been successful? This forces students to redefine the meaning of success for themself, and gives them opportunities to express opinions, and increases their perceptions of their fellow students.

48. A Person I would like someday to become

Procedures:

1. Explain to the class that people often have in their mind a vision of what they would like to become.
2. Ask students to write how they are now closer to that vision. They might want to mention past or future life experiences that did or would have helped to prepare them for what they want to become.
3. Students whould also include what they still need to do to become that person in the future.

49. Favorite characters

Procedures:

1. Ask students to choose a book in which they would like to be the main character.
2. Either discuss or have the students write why they chose that character. This will show what students admire, what their aspirations are, and what they consider successful.

50. For the sports-minded

Procedures:

Follow any of the suggested activities:

1. Write and illustrate an informal book about sports.
2. Read books about sports — famous players, history.
3. Use sports words to study vocabulary and spelling.
4. Draw pictures to illustrate sports events.
5. Write poems about the subject.
6. Use math skills to calculate averages, records, etc.

51. Success notebooks

Procedures:

> At the end of each day, students write down one successful experience that happened that day and why they thought it was successful. (Can be done as class project. Instead of individual notebooks, class can participate in success of the day.)

52. "This is your life"

Procedures:

1. A school employee such as a custodian, secretary, etc., is chosen as a star of the event at a school assembly or class meeting.
2. Students must then collect successful and happy experiences from this person's life.
3. Presentation of collected memorabilia to "star" at event.

Materials:

> Pictures, souvenirs, stories.

53. Ladder of success

Procedures:

1. Each Student draws a ladder of success.
2. On each rung the child writes something related to success. For example: What does success mean to you? What do you need to be successful? What do you do well? (As an alternative, Students can write successful experiences over a designated period of time.)

54. Analyzing and comparing successes in history

Procedures:

> Students can have a discussion about success for different people in different areas at different times. How does the idea of success differ according to economic and geographic changes?

55. Neighborhood workers

Procedures:

1. Prepare students by discussing the types of jobs available in the neighborhood and their importance to the people in the community.
2. Have neighborhood workers visit class to discuss their jobs (how they got it, qualifications, job description).

Materials:

> Workers from various positions in neighborhood (contact parents and relatives for volunteers).

CHAPTER THREE

Tapping and actualizing students' strengths

We live in times of great power: atomic power, the power of nationalism, black power, the power of mass media, and the power to get men to the moon and back. We are all aware of these manifestations of power; we are all affected by them. Too many of us, however, are too little aware of its origin. Fundamentally, every such manifestation of power is rooted in the individual. To a very large extent, individuals derive their great power from the utilization of their many strengths.

Each individual is unique because he/she has different strengths and capacities. Too often, however, people are unaware of their strengths and operate on only a few of them. An unidentified strength is all too often an unused strength.

Strengths refer to any skill, ability, talent or personal trait that help people express themselves or to function more productively in their world. Specifically, strengths are powers — powers to act in a variety of areas — physical, intellectual, creative, emotional, and vocational. However, in order for any skill or trait to become a strength, it must be activated. Individuals must have opportunities to see and experience their own strengths. When people recognize that they have unique strengths they like themselves more and their self-image is greatly enhanced.

The classroom is the natural place for students to begin to understand their potentials and to actualize them. Teachers become "strength facilitators" setting the atmosphere, designing the tasks, and identifying and developing the strengths of their students. Toward these ends, here are some general techniques to keep in mind:

- To compliment a child on gaining something, give out awards. For example, to encourage neatness and good handwriting, a handwriting award designed like a diploma can be given to the children who correctly form all their letters and who complete their work neatly.

- Many times children reveal themselves in their writing. Reinforce those strengths that are revealed in the written composition. Point out other strengths that you have observed but which, perhaps, the child was unaware of, and try to alter any negative aspects of the self-concept.

- When setting up the lesson plans for the week, write the names of particular children you want to pay attention to and compliment in your plan book.

- Whenever possible, allow for choice in assignments or in the way the tasks may be completed. This will increase motivation and allow for individual creativity.

- When handing back written work, put specific positive comments, not just a grade.

Remember that each student has academic as well as personal strengths (see the chart below for some examples). It is the responsibility of the teacher to utilize all available potential.

Early Childhood/Elementary School

56. Activities to Maximize Individual Academic and Personal Strengths

STRENGTH	ACTIVITY
Good Memory	Be a prompter in the school plays. Help to drill the words to songs in music class. Help in spelling and math drills. Act as a resource for remembering rules to games.
Articulate	Serve as a spokesman for class in presentation of project or activity to an audience. Serve as leader in classroom discussion or small group discussions. Relate a creative story verbally rather than writing it. Serve as a beginner for group-developed story. Relay messages from teachers to others. Narrate class play.
Artistic	Work on bulletin boards for class, covering different subject areas being studied. Design colorful, artistic designs and signs for the room. Help other students with their drawing when they need to illustrate a report. Help in drawing pictures for murals.
Math	Plan budget for a class party. Be class treasurer. Write out the attendance report. Make up problems pertaining to the classroom, e.g., perimeter and area of the room.
Science	Demonstrate an experiment for the class. Have rock collections.

	Have rock collections.
Leadership	Chairman of committee.
	Officer of the class.
	Team captain in athletics.
	Teaching songs.
Friendliness	Establish welcoming committee to introduce
& Warmth	new children and include them in class activities.
Responsibility	Give out jobs and tasks.

57. Love Letters

Procedures:

1. Children decorate brown paper lunch bags "valentine" style and place their names on them.
2. These are "mailboxes" that are hung up on the bulletin board.
3. During the month the children create "valentine gifts" which reflect the things they like about their classmates and "deliver" them to the mailboxes.
4. The teacher should monitor mailboxes to make sure that each child gets a note. If not, the teacher should write a note for that child and put it in the mailbox.

Materials:

brown lunch bags

58. Be a teacher

Procedures:

1. With the cooperation of lower grade teachers send older students to help younger students with their work. For example, they can help with math, reading, and writing. They can also become a story teller or share their own stories with primary classes.
2. Art teachers, gym teachers, music teachers, or any other special area teachers can be included.

59. Adjectives

Procedures:

1. Students use the dictionary to select and make a list of the adjectives that describe themselves.

2. Ask the class to form into pairs of students. The members of the pair exchange their lists of self descriptive adjectives. Each person puts a check mark next to the adjectives which pertain to both of them (which he/she agree describes the other person?).

3. Each person reads the checked adjectives aloud to the other person and gives the evidence to prove that the adjective truly applies.

(A variation of this idea is to give the students a list of adjectives and have them check off those which apply to both themselves and their classmates.)

LIST OF ADJECTIVES

Reliable	Affectionate	Neat
Trustworthy	Even-tempered	Enthusiastic
Helpful	Refined	Loyal
Earnest	Organized	Optimistic
Straightforward	Calm	Just
Sincere	Courageous	Honest
Kind	Brave	Hopeful
Polite	Loving	Beautiful
Ambitious	Grateful	Original
Faithful	Generous	Unique
Truthful	Peaceful	Respectful
Moral	Humorous	Pure

Materials:

Dictionary

60. Strengths

Procedures:

1. Put all the students' names in a box and ask everyone to select a name.
2. Then, each student must describe aloud one positive physical or behavioral trait of the person whose name they drew.
3. The members of the class try to discover the person whose traits are being described.
4. Some of the students may guess incorrectly. This does not necessarily mean that the classmate they chose does not have that trait. Inevitably some, possibly many, students will share the same trait(s).

61. Friendship Chain

Procedures:

1. Write the name of a friend on each chain link.
2. Write one positive word that describes your friend.
3. Cut out the chain links and staple them together.
4. Add your chain links to those of your schoolmates in order to form a class friendship chain.
5. Hang the chain in you classroom.

Materials:

Pencils, crayons, construction paper

62. Cinquain Poetry

Procedures:

1. Introduce the structure of Cinquain poetry.
   Line 1 - noun
   Line 2 - two adjectives describing the noun.
   Line 3 - three verbs ending in "ing" that describe the noun.
   Line 4 - thought about the noun.
   Line 5 - synonym for the noun.
2. After children understand the structure, have them write poems about themselves. This can also be a whole class effort using the blackboard, each class member contributing to the poems.
   For example:
     John is
     funny, strong
     caring, understanding, listening,
     an excellent soccer player
     friend
3. When the class or individuals complete poems, they can mount them on construction paper and draw a background that describes them. An example can be a soccer field or a classroom or a beach etc.
4. You can share poems, display them in the classroom, in the hallway or publish a collective book including all the children's poems and distribute to the class.

63. Personalized Bulletin Boards

Procedures:

Have bulletin board reflect the individuality and personal feelings of the students. Examples:

- Have a "student of the week" board devoted to one student each week. He/she may put up any items, pictures, and/or writings about himself/herself or others.
- Have a "Brag Board" for a month on which each student puts up a "commercial" about himself/herself.

64. Our Neighborhood Diorama

Procedures:

1. Take a walk around our school neighborhood. Have the children note and discuss all that they see: cars, signs, roads, stores, homes, foliage, landscaping, people, community workers, unusual sights, an so on.
2. Construct "Our Neighborhood Model". Each child contributes what he/she is good at to the end product. The whole class will work on this together, each doing a different phase; painting, constructing, gluing, cutting, making scenery, buildings, people, etc.
3. Set up the display in the hallway alcove outside our room. Have a chart behind the table noting what each child contributed to the project.

Materials:

Building materials (cartons, blocks, legos, etc.), paints, glue, cardboard, a large table to put everything on.

65. "We are wonderful cartoon"

Procedure:

Have the entire class collaborate on a story about how wonderful we are. The children can be the illustrators: every child will get a 12" section of the butcher paper. Roll it out on the floor and let a few children at a time work on their own sections. Children can draw their own pictures and illustrate their good qualities, then sign their name on the bottom of their picture section. Everyone contributes. The cartoon is rolled from one dowel to the other - an open side of the box serving as a theater screen.

Materials:

Large cardboard box for a theater, two wooden dowels that are 6" taller than the carton, paints, crayons, a long roll of butcher paper.

66. My culture is special

Procedures: Have a United Nations Day!

1. Have children interview parents, relatives, or friends born in another country, and use the interview as a bulletin board entitled "Waves of Immigration". The interview will be written on paper shaped like a boat. The flag of the individual's country of origin will be placed above it.

2. Have children make a family tree of great grandparents, grandparents, parents and themselves.

3. On U.N. day, children will share one aspect of their culture. They may teach the class a traditional dance; share words or phrases from their mother language; bring in money from that part of the world; wear traditional dress, share customary foods etc. Children with American backgrounds will focus on typically American customs, foods etc.

67. Something I did well today

Procedures:

1. Create a bulletin board entitled "Something I Did Well Today" (or "This Week").
2. Display the work that a child is proud of.

68. Mirror reflection

Procedures:

Children imagine themselves looking in a mirror and then describe their positive qualities.

69. "Strength chair"

Procedures:

1. A student sits in the "strength chair".
2. The student tells about his/her positive strengths.
3. The class then adds to these strengths and tells what they like about the student and why

Materials:

A decorated chair or desk.

70. Gingerbread men

Procedures:

1. On each gingerbread man write an obvious strength for each child without writing the child's name. Place a number on each form.
2. Place all the gingerbread men in an oven (box).
3. Announce to the children that you did some baking last night and made some gingerbread men.
4. Explain to the children that each gingerbread man has a number and something special written on it. each gingerbread man matches someone in the class.
5. Children should then try to match the gingerbread men to the students. (There isn't any wrong answer. Children possess more than one quality.)

Materials:

Construction paper to create a gingerbread man for each child.

71. Why is this person famous?

Procedures:

1. Show a picture of a famous person to the class.
2. Ask the class to discuss what strengths made the person famous.
3. Place the picture on the bulletin board.
4. The teacher or a student can write the information contributed by the class on an index card under the photo.

72. Class book

Procedures:

1. Have each student write a page about themself describing their good experiences, likes, ambitions, etc.
2. Collect the pages from all the students and bind them into a book.
3. The book is then available for the students to view at their leisure.

Materials:

Photos, paper, pens/pencils

73. Awards program

Procedures:

1. At the end of the year, have an awards program.
2. Let the students vote for who gets the awards e.g., friendliest, good ball player, monitor.
3. Each student will get an award for a recognized strength

Materials:

Award for each student in class

74. Mix and match strengths

Procedures:

1. Have children write strengths on individual pieces of paper.
2. The teacher writes the strengths on the blackboard.
3. Let the class decide which children possess the strengths on the blackboard

75. "I Can" scrapbook

Procedures:

1. Children draw pictures of themselves performing their own special talents.
2. On their own, or with help, strengths are identified and placed on paper.
3. Children create a book and share it with the class stressing their uniqueness.

Materials:

Drawing paper, crayons, markers, drawing pencils, fasteners

76. Self-concept puppets

Procedures:

1. Children create puppets in the image of themselves.
2. Children create TV commercial to sell the puppet stressing all the wonderful things it can do.

Materials:

Socks, buttons, glue, yearn, bric-a-brac, big box cut to resemble TV

77. Steppingstones

Procedures:

1. Children draw pictures of their strengths.
2. Teacher collects pictures and scatters them on the floor. The width of the classroom is a brook.
3. Each child gets to step on (strength) stepping-stone in order to cross the brook (classroom).
4. Children learn that the utilization of strengths helps to achieve goals.

Materials:

Drawing paper, crayons/pencils/markers

78. King or queen for a day

Procedures:

1. Appoint a child king or queen for a day.
2. Child is asked to explain how he/she will use his/her special talents, strengths, abilities, to be a wise ruler.

Materials:

Crown

79. Choices

Procedures:

Within the room have different areas a child can go to, such as art, music, blocks, science, math, library, games, etc. Watch the children; ask questions and give praise; communicate with them. By providing many interest areas you can find out the child's strengths and encourage decision making. In order for children to develop their strength potentials they must practice them and feel they are valued. Children can choose their own activity from two or three alternatives — this encourages decision making, provides motivation and engenders the sense that their decisions are valued.

80. Why people like me

Procedures:

Have each child make a book called "Why People Like Me." It develops a positive self-concept because the individual sees that there are certain strengths which enhance his/her popularity.

81. Compliments stepladder

Procedures:

Children mark each step with some compliment they received that day, thus making children more aware of their strengths.

Materials:

Mimeograph of a picture of a stepladder for each child.

82. Good deed box

Procedures:

Ask children to write an anonymous note that tells about something nice they saw someone doing during the day and put the note in the deed box. Teacher can read the contents of this box at the end of each day.

Materials:

Box labeled "Good Deeds"

83. Pin the strength on the donkey

Procedures:

Set up a huge picture of "Pin the Tail on the Donkey" and divide into several major areas of strengths. Each child makes a tag with the name of his/her skill. The children then pin their strength tags on the proper area of the donkey.

Materials:

Large cardboard cutout donkey, tags or post-its

84. Let's make a strength

Procedures:

Let's make a strength (like "Let's Make a Deal"). One child is emcee and is giving away strengths. Other children have play money and try to buy strengths they would like to have.

Materials:

Cardboard cut outs each containing a strength on it, play money

85. Individual or small-group activities

Procedures:

1. Crossword puzzle: Have each child make a crossword puzzle using words about his strengths.
2. Tic-Tac-Toe: Instead of X and O, use each child's strengths.
3. Hang-Man: Make up words about strengths only.
4. Poems: Each child writes a poem about how he/she sees himself.
5. Riddles: Have each child make up a riddle about one of his/her strengths. The class must guess who the person is.

86. Variety show

Procedures:

Children will display their various talents — those which they feel successful at. For example, children who feel they are funny and have a good sense of humor will show their strength by telling jokes. There is no talent or personal attribute that is so minor that it should be overlooked. There should be a place for every child in the talent show.

Materials:

Stage area, costumes & props if desired

87. Class newspaper

Procedures:

A class newspaper can use many strengths: editors - children who are good at organization and writing; reporters - those who are accurate and observant; illustrators - class artists; cartoons, jokes - the class comedian.

Subjects covered can include every area of the curriculum; poems, stories, science experiments, puzzling math problems, word jumbles (the best speller can use spelling words), crossword puzzles, biographies or autobiographies (this can be used to increase the students' self-image as well as to help the children to know one another better).

Materials:

Paper, pens/pencils, print shop or access to photocopy machine

88. Making books

Procedures:

> This may be either an individual or a group activity. The children can either write their own stories, rewrite a familiar tale, or cover a specific subject area. Many strengths are utilized in planning, organizing, designing, illustrating, writing, and binding the books.

89. Bulletin board displays

Procedures:

> Given a topic and guidelines with which to work, the class can be divided into small groups each assigned to create a bulletin board display. Many strengths will be employed. A child with leadership qualities can direct and coordinate the activities. A child with good research skills can scan books, magazines and encyclopedias for information. A child who writes well can write the reports, poems or stories. A child who is artistically inclined can prepare the illustrations, maps, or charts. Children will be needed to set up displays and to staple the material to the board. There is a strength to fit every task.

Materials:

> Art supplies, paper, colored paper, pens, pencils, crayons, markers, etc.
>
> Reference materials - books, magazines, encyclopedias.

90. Class monitors

Procedures:

Letting children be class monitors provides them with many strength opportunities. First, relying on children for a given task helps develop responsibility and leadership skills.

91. Fortune cookies

Procedures:

This is a double task. First, a math lesson can be incorporated into teaching measurements for making the cookies. Then the children can write fortunes - ones that they would consider good fortunes. When you read each individual fortune, it may help you to identify some of the students' strengths. The cookies will be exchanged in class.

Materials:

Recipe ingredients, use of oven, paper, pen.

92. An informal personality profile

Procedures:

These instruments can be used to probe for a child's strengths.
- Informal questioning, written or oral: What do you like to do best? What don't you like to do? Why?
- Open ended sentences: I feel good when I ...., My best subject is ...., My father makes me happiest when he ....
- Drawing pictures illustrating a favorite interest.

93. Class fair

Procedures:

> Have children contribute projects on subjects they're interested in. Invite other classes come in to see your work.

94. Penmanship

Procedures:

> Children with the best handwriting write assignments on the blackboard, write class letters of thanks, get-well notes, or signs for bulletin boards.

95. "This is your life"

Procedure:

> Choose a different child each week. The class gives the child's strengths and the child adds his/her own. Make a scrapbook or posters with pictures and a list of strengths and hang it on the wall .

Materials:

> Paper, pens, pencils, markers, poster board, pictures (magazines/personal).

96. Peer-group teaching

Procedures:

> Set aside time during the day to have children teach or demonstrate some individual skill or talents they might possess - anything from making a paper airplane to explaining a mathematical equation. Reciprocal learning will take place; each person becomes a teacher in one area and a student in another. This reciprocity encourage individual success and a feeling of worth and value.

97. Panel game

Procedures:

1. A panel of children (perhaps three or four) sit at the front of the room and secretly pick a child in the room (no one in the class knows who, not even the child picked).
2. The panel must describe the child (without using physical descriptions) with descriptions such as: he/she is very friendly and easy to get along with, he/she is good in art, he/she is smart, etc. (only positive attributes are allowed.)
3. The class must guess who the panel has chosen.

98. People I admire

Procedures:

1. Have your students cut out the pictures of people they admire.
2. Under each picture have the quality that they most admire about this person they selected.
3. As an additional assignment you can have your class write and list what they can do to achieve those qualities they admire in the people they selected.

Materials:

Magazines, scissors, paper, glue

99. Making up a story

Procedures:

1. Have the children sit around in a circle. Tell them they are going to make up their own story.
2. Start off by saying "What I like to do best is ". Encourage the children to continue the story.

   Most children enjoy talking about themselves and their experiences, and at the same time they will be giving you valuable information that you can use later.

100. Literary "Concentration"

Procedures:

Have each child make a deck of cards. One half of the cards will identify authors. The identification can be a picture, dates of birth/death, the titles of one or more books, or a combination of these and other biographical datum. The other half of the deck will contain a card for each author that lists particular strengths or positive qualities with which the author is associated. Break the students into small groups. Each group will tthen play the game of "Concentration" using one member of the groups deck of cards. The cards are turned face down and each student takes turns choosing two, hoping they will match. When two cards match, the student keeps the pair of cards and gets another turn. The student with the most pairs at the end wins.

101. For the good writer

Procedures:

1. Encourage a good writer to keep a daily or weekly log of classroom activities, projects, etc.
2. Have the student organize a class newspaper.
3. Have the student enter writing or essay contests.
4. Allow the student to help compose notices to be sent home to parents, to other teachers, etc.

102. Famous class quotations

Procedures:

1. Keep a record of things people say in class.
2. Make a book of "Famous Class Quotations".
3. Under each quote write the student's name.

103. TV show parodies

Procedures:

Organize some typical game shows where a panel of children try to guess a particular strength of a classmate through questioning. Some possible games are:
"What's My Strength/Success"
"I've Got a Strength/Success"
"To Tell the Strength/Success"

104. Positive feedback

Procedure:

Make positive, specific statements on their report cards, at parent-teacher conferences, and directly to the student.

105. Positive qualities in a name

Procedures:

1. Children write each letter of their name on a separate index card.
2. On each card the children write a positive quality that starts with that letter. For example,
   S - sensitive
   A - ambitious
   M - masculine
3. Children can also list positive qualities of parents, siblings, friends, teachers, etc. using the initials of their names.

Materials:

index cards

106. Circle games

Procedures:

1. Have the children sit in a circle.
2. Pose some introductory phrases like "I like myself because ...", "I am proud of myself because ...", etc.
3. Let the children complete the phrases.

107. Strength notebook

Procedures:

1. Children have their own strength notebook.
2. At the end of each day they write down a particular strength that they used that day and how it helped them.

Materials:

notebook, pen

108. Developing a strength

Procedures:

1. Children can set a daily, weekly or monthly goal that requires them to develop a new strength.
2. They can report on their progress periodically.

109. Future children

Procedures:

1. Ask the children to sit on the floor in the circle.
2. Elicit from the children the various qualities that they like about themselves.
3. Have the class brainstorm about the qualities that the children would like their own children to possess.
4. Discuss why those qualities are important to have.

110. Best friends

Procedures:

1. Ask the children to bring in a picture of their best friend.
2. Give each child a piece of chart paper.
3. Each child will paste their friend's picture at the top of the paper. Children without a picture may draw one at the top of the paper.
4. Under the picture the children will list the positive qualities that they like about the friend .
5. The children will take turns going up to the front of the classroom. As each child displays the chart and reads the qualities, he/she will be asked to give reasons why they like that particular quality.

Materials:

Chart paper, Magic markers, Pictures of friends

111. Grab bag of strengths

Procedures:

1. Have the children write a strength on a card.
2. Put the cards in a grab bag and have each child role-play the strength that he/she has picked.
3. Fellow classmates try to guess what the strength is.

Materials:

paper, pen, brown bag

112. The helping hand

Procedures:

1. The teacher chooses a Helping Hand (a teacher assistant to help with various class tasks.) Each day a new child is chosen so everyone gets a chance to shine as the teacher's helper.
2. The teacher makes a point at the end of the day to thank the assistant for helping, and then has the other children in the class reiterate all the valuable things the helper did during the day.

Materials:

Large, colorful felt hand print mounted on a bulletin board, cards in a box with each child's name on it.

113. Me book

Procedures:

1. Have the children design a book cover. Each cover should have the child's picture in a frame. The title would read: *Me Fabulous Me*
2. The child would complete or illustrate the following statements:

I am special because...
The best day I ever had was...
My best subject is...
I am a good friend because...
I helped my mother/father when...
My favorite hobby is...
Right now I'm not good at , but I can get better by...
Here is something else you should know about me...

Materials:

A photograph of each child, construction paper, crayons or markers, glue.

114. My inner-self

Procedures:

1. Children will write an entry into their daily journal. They may wish to make it a private diary or may wish to share at least some of the events and feelings written.
2. "Circle of Love" will take place each morning as soon as the class arrives and settles down for the new day. Children may share an entry from their journal, a feeling they may presently have, and/or a recent event or occurrence at home.
3. Write a personal message to each child at least once a week that focuses on one strength that they recently exhibited in school.
4. Have a class song that encourages students to persevere.
   For example,
   Try, try, try again,
   Try again and see,
   Don't give up and try again,
   And finally succeed.

115. Charts for children

Procedures:

1. Give each student a piece of construction paper. Have them draw a line three inches from the top of the paper. In that three inch space tell them to write their name, preceded by one positive adjective.

2. The rest of the paper is left blank and all of the student papers are hung on the wall. Each day, the students write the strengths of their classmates on the charts.

3. This provides an opportunity for children to recognize both their peer's and their own strengths.

116. Power list

Procedures:

1. Children write their name at the top of a piece of paper.
2. Teacher collects papers and redistributes them, making sure each child receives a different person's paper.
3. Students write something they like about the person whose name is at the top.
4. Teacher collects papers and redistributes as before.
5. Repeat process several times.
6. Return papers to correct children and let them read what was written about them.

117. Personal Bingo

Procedures:

1. The bingo board has sixteen boxes on which each student will have the chance to list sixteen strengths. The list of strengths will be obtained from a list the teacher hands out.
2. Each student will receive sixteen index cards. With markers, the children will write one strength on each card.

3. The students will receive a bingo board sheet. They will fill in each box with a strength.
4. Collect the cards and put them in a bag. Collect the bingo board sheets.
5. Randomly hand out the sheets and bingo chips (not to the owners).
6. Draw from the collection of cards and play Personal Bingo. (Four across, up and down, or diagonally will win.)
7. The person with the winning sheet has to try to match the strengths on the bingo board to the child who has these strengths.
8. Play for several rounds.

Materials:

Copies of blank bingo board, bingo chips, thin markers, small index cards cut in half, white labels, chart paper.

118. Tap your strengths

Procedures:

1. Students are given a list of 10 positive characteristics i.e. kind, smart, funny, warm, caring, understanding, good memory, good artist, energetic and honest. Other strengths can be used. They are told to write the names of classmates that have the characteristics listed.
2. Children are told to put their heads down on their desks. The teacher taps the children he/she feels possess at least one of the listed characteristics.
3. The teacher taps all the children.
4. Children will raise heads and discuss how they felt when they were tapped.

119. Lucky leprechaun

Procedures:

1. Each child traces and cuts out a large shamrock and prints his/her name clearly on the front.
2. The shamrocks are placed *name facing in* toward the bulletin board with thumb tacks.
3. Each day one shamrock is removed and turned around. The person whose name appears on the shamrock is the "Lucky Leprechaun."
4. The other children create pretty drawings or works of art to either place on the bulletin board or give to the "Lucky Leprechaun."
5. At the end of the day the "Lucky Leprechaun" takes the shamrock and "creations" home.

120. Interview for strengths

Procedures:

1. Children will sit in pairs and interview each other. They will ask each other about their favorite subjects, their hobbies, and what they are good at doing.
2. Children will decide what they like best about their classmates' qualities. They will write sentences about each other. For example, "*John* is special because he is smart."
3. Students will draw portraits of each other engaged in activities they enjoy.
4. The class will gather. Children will hold their own portrait and say why they are special to their friend.

121. Friendship tree

Procedures:

1. "Our Friendship Tree" will be displayed.
2. Students write strengths of their classmates on each leaf of the tree.
3. Leaves of the tree will include all the qualities students found to be special in their classmates.

Materials:

Paper, crayons

122. All about me

Procedures:

1. *Yesterday*
   Children will bring in baby pictures at the beginning of the school term. They will be put on the bulletin board and a "*Guess Who*?" contest will follow. Under each picture students will write a clue about themselves. They will also write something they are good at or like to do.
2. *Today*
   During mid-term, pictures of various school activities will be displayed. Each child will be in at least one picture. Each child in the picture will write a sentence telling how the particular activity made them feel. I felt ...because...
3. *Tomorrow*
   At the end of the term, children will make hats that depict what they want to do in the future. They will each tell the class about one strength they have that would make them good at the profession they have chosen.
   Pictures will be taken and displayed and captions will read: "I will be a ...when I grow up because I am good at ...".

Materials:

Baby photo for each child, photographs of this year's school activities, paper hats

123. Puzzle match game

Procedures:

1. For each student, cut a piece of cardboard in half so they fit like a puzzle.
2. On one half of a piece of cardboard print the child's name and on the other half write or draw his/her specific strength.
   For example:
   Vincent - singer
   Kenneth - artist
   Lucio - soccer player
   Lauren - reader
   Michael - fast runner
3. Students must match the child's strengths with his/her name. The two cardboard puzzle pieces will only fit together for the correct child. The children get to see something great about everyone in the class.

Materials:

Two interlocking puzzle pieces made from cardboard for each student.

124. I am special T-shirt

Procedures:

1. Provide the class with paint and brushes. Tell them to paint "I Am Special" diagonally across the front and on the other side to paint words, sentences, or pictures of things that make them special. For example: baseball team, good in math, speaks another language.

2.   The children should be encouraged to wear these to a class assembly, on their birthday, or on any day they feel they want to. This will increase awareness of their strengths.

Materials:

One light-colored T-shirt per child, paint, paint brushes

125. Strength & skill swap

Procedures:

1.   Divide the class into pairs. They will team up to teach each other something.
2.   Post a chart with the strengths the children will swap. For example:
     Strength & Skill Swap
     Erica: sewing
     Lauren: dancing
     Dennis: pitching a baseball
     Kenneth: Drawing cartoons
     Mary: cutting paper dolls
     Jennifer: weaving on a loom
     Jack: making paper mache
     Christine: origami
3.   Give each team member a chance to demonstrate what skill they have learned from the other partner. This can be done during show and tell.

126. I'm special and so is my family

Procedures:

1.   Children will make a self-portrait from the shoulders up. Yarn will be used for hair. Other features and clothing parts will be made of construction paper. Under each portrait, on a slip of paper, children will write their names and reasons why they are special.
2.   Children will make a house out of construction paper. They will draw faces of family members peeking out the

windows. Under each house, on a slip of paper, the children will write their family names and a reason why their families are special.

3. The first bulletin board will say. "I am special and..." and will display the portraits. The second one would say, "... so is my family!" and would display the houses.

Materials:

Construction paper, glue, scissors, brown, black and yellow yarn.

127. Class quilt

Procedures:

1. The children will break into groups of four. In the groups, they will name and give evidence for strengths in themselves and the others in the group.
2. Children will choose the strength that they feel is the one that best represents them.
3. On one white square, children will use fabric crayons to write their names and draw a symbol for the strength.
4. Children will complete a quilt square by backing their own strength square with batting and another white square. They will sew these pieces together and display the class quilt of strengths.

Materials:

Solid squares (about 6 inches by 6 inches) of white fabric batting, needles, thread, fabric crayons.

128. Positive behavior reward coupons

Procedures:

1. Make a set of coupons or awards. You can use rubber stamps, stickers, pictures from magazines, comics, anything that will reproduce on a Xerox machine. (You may also want to use ditto paper if it is more convenient to use in your school.)
2. Some titles for coupons could be, "You did a great job today on ...", "You helped the class by ...", "You were very thoughtful when you ...", or any other situation that applies to your classroom.
3. Remember, only one set has to be made because it can be reproduced over and over again.
4. Make sure you keep track of the people you give the coupons to. Very often some students get overlooked. Give out at least one coupon per day.
5. Send notices to the parents when children receive a coupon, so the parents can also reinforce their strengths at home.

Materials:

Teacher made coupons/awards, or store bought coupons/awards

129. The strengths of planet Earth

Procedures:

1. Have children close their eyes and imagine traveling to another planet.
2. Children must decide what planet they want to travel to.
3. Tell children that they will meet aliens on the planet.
4. In a paragraph, they must tell the aliens five positive things they like about Planet Earth and give the reasons that they like these things.

130. Acrostic poem

Procedures:

1. Explain the structure for writing an acrostic poem.
2. Have them use the names of their classmates to create a "strengths acrostic poem".
3. This can be done as a whole class lesson or an individual lesson.
   Example:
   J olly
   O penminded
   H andy
   N ature lover
4. This is a great lesson in which to use a thesaurus.
5. You can also decorate with markers and display in the classroom or in the hallway.

131. Bag of Strengths

Procedures:

1. Divide the class into two groups.
2. The children in the first group are told to take their plastic "strength" bags with them, and stand in front of the classroom.
3. The children in the other group are told "Each child standing in front of the room has certain strengths. You are going to write each of their strengths on separate pieces of paper." (The teacher gives an example.)
4. Now, one at a time, each child in the group standing at the front of the room repeats his/her name. All the children in the other group write as many strengths as they can think of (on separate pieces of paper) for the child who has just spoken.
5. When they've finished writing the strengths, the children all walk up to the child and put the pieces of paper with

the "Strengths" which he has recorded into the child's "Strength Bag". Then the bag is sealed with a rubber band.

6. When each child in the first group has a filled sealed bag, the groups switch roles.

Materials:

One baggie and rubber band per child

132. The Musical Chair Strength Game

Procedures:

1. One child is picked by the teacher to name as many strengths as he can about another child.
2. The strengths and the name of the child being spoken about are recorded on the blackboard.
3. For each strength recorded, a chair is added into the circle.
4. The more strengths said, the more chairs the teacher adds into the circle until all of the chairs are in the center of the classroom.
5. The teacher puts on the record player.
6. Children sing the strengths of that child to music.
7. Repeat this procedure for each child.

Materials:

Chairs, record player, record album

Junior High/High School

133. Collage

Procedures:

1. Students choose one classmate as their subject and write down all the positive qualities that characterize that student.
2. They then have to leaf through magazines finding pictures that represent these qualities, and make a collage representing that person.

Materials:

Paper, pens, glue scissors, magazines

134. Imaginary trip

Procedures:

1. Students will decide on a place that would provide an environment where they feel they could be most successful. For example, students may want to go to the Amazon because they feel successful meeting challenging situations.
2. In an even broader context this imaginary trip can include world, national or local problems that the students feel they will be most successful at solving.
3. This eventually can be limited to a narrower scope where students will be able to set real,personal goals that can be achieved within the classroom or at home.

Materials:

paper, pen (if done as a writing activity)

135. Imagery painting

Procedures:

1. Assign colors and symbols to certain strengths.
2. Students choose a strength they would like to possess. Then, they do a monochromatic painting of any object they feel best describes the strength chosen.
   Example - The student decides that blue equals a responsible person. The student then may paint a landscape in blue with various shades and tints. An oak tree could be the center of the landscape. The oak tree would represent strength.

Materials:

paper, paint, paint brushes, cups, water, paper towels

136. One-man shows

Procedures:

1. Set aside a small part of an art class each day in which students can pick five to ten art projects that they feel are successful. Have them give a one man show for that day, displaying the projects.
2. You may also have students make a poster advertising themselves before the show. This builds a positive self-image.

Materials:

Portfolio containing works done by each child.

137. Favorite historical person

Procedures:

> Have members of the class pick a person in history and make a collage or poster showing why they like the person chosen.

Materials:

> magazines, paints, glue, scissors, paper

138. Country identification

Procedures:

1. Have students draw a picture of the country they feel they most resemble (e.g., the U.S. because it's powerful, etc.)
2. All the countries are then arranged to form a map, expressing the idea that every whole is made up of unique parts, each of which have some strengths.

Materials:

> paper, markers

139. Past, Present and Future Success

Procedures:

1. Verbs tenses will be used to illustrate past present and future successes.
2. The past or present tense can be learned by having students tell what they felt their successes and strengths were five years ago.
3. To learn the present tense, they can tell what their successes and strengths are today.
4. Likewise, they can explore the future tense by predicting what their successes and strengths will be.

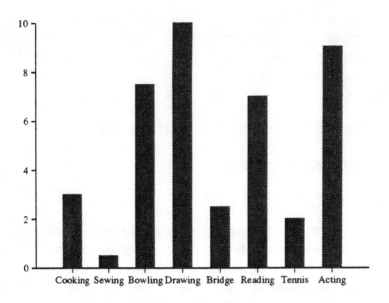

140. Bar Graph of Achievements

Procedures:

Ask students to list their hobbies and achievements on a bar graph. See the example above. Record hobbies on the horizontal axis. Label the vertical axis from 1 to ten and then assign the degree of achievement in each hobby a value from 1 to 10. Draw a bar up the vertical axis for each hobby. This technique enables the students to visualize their achievements from a perspective that induces feelings of pride and confidence.

141. I like me

Procedures:

1. Have the class set up a theorem beginning "I Like myself because . . . .".
2. Have them create a step by step proof for their theorem.

142. Asymptote

Procedures:

Ask the class to write a paper on "What Asymptotically Approaches Perfection About Me." Like human efforts to achieve perfection, it infinitely approaches a level, but will never reach it. Here the teacher can find out in what areas the student strives for perfection.

143. Student math teachers

Procedures:

Ask students to explore some aspect of math that they are good at and to teach some new facet of it to the class.

144. Vector representations

Procedures:

After the topic on vectors (symbols for forces that show both magnitude and direction), ask students to describe a vector representation of themselves. They should consider the forces behind them. What personal strength gives them magnitude? In what direction are they pointed?

145. How therapists use strengths

Procedures:

1. Have the students read one of the two assigned books.
2. Ask the students what the contributing factors to Dibs' or Debbie's recovery were. Have them describe how the therapist brought out their strengths.

Materials:

Hanna Green's *I Never Promised You a Rose Garden* or Virginia Axline's *Dibs*

146. Sons and lovers

Procedures:

1. Have the students read the book and then describe Paul's strength potentials.
2. How were these potentials developed? What specific people and situations contributed to the development of these strengths.

Materials:

Sons and Lovers

147. Student autobiographies

Procedures:

1. Ask the students to write their autobiographies, describing the years of their development.
2. They should try especially to remember people and incidents that contributed to the development of their strengths.
3. Encourage them to be honest with themselves. For example, if they write well, they should ask themselves who originally encouraged them to write.

148. As others see us ...

Procedures:

1. Ask students to choose one person (family or friend) and describe his/her strengths.
2. They should ask this person what he/she considers to be his/her most valuable strengths and compare views.
3. Sometimes there is a discrepancy between the way people view themselves and the way others view them. If this happens, the two can discuss why they chose a particular strength.

149. "Jeopardy"

Procedures:

1. Use the TV game of "Jeopardy" as a review at the end of a literature class.
2. The game questions can be broken into categories, such as biographies, styles, characters.
3. Students choose to devise the questions, or enact some role such as judges, scorekeepers, stage builder, quiz master or contestants. Students will volunteer for what they feel most capable of doing.

150. Poem interpretations

Procedures:

1. Have students select a poem to interpret, using whatever means they choose.
2. The student might create another poem, a song, an interpretive dance or some artistic creation.

Materials:

Various poems.

151. Recreating historical events

Procedures:

1. Set up groups, and assign students with leadership qualities to be group leaders.
2. The groups would recreate events in history. The students will choose to represent historical characters with whom they feel a kinship.

152. Help wanted bulletin

Procedures:

1. Students write want ads and resumes describing their strengths.
2. They can also try to sell their good qualities to their classmates who act as prospective employers.

153. Sign in please

Procedures:

1. Place a large bulletin board on a wall in the room.
2. Each student signs in on a daily basis.
3. Have them write a sentence about something they did well that day.

154. Guess my strength and career

Procedures:

1. Ask the students to think of something that they like to do or something good about themselves. Then, ask them to think of a job that they could perform using this special trait. Give the class several examples (e.g., one may be adept with pastels and could become an artist; or one may be a very understanding person who wants to help others and could become a good guidance counselor).

2. Give them the rules of the game. One student will come to the front of the room; the rest of the class will try to guess the strength and the career the student has chosen. Start at one end of the room. Give each individual in turn the opportunity to ask a question that requires a yes or no response. If the question gets a "yes" response that person can ask another question. If no one is able to guess the strength and career after everyone has asked at least one question, the student who is up front can reveal the answer.

155. Sell Yourself

Procedures:

1. Discuss with the class the criteria of a good advertisement. Try to elicit that a good advertisement captures your attention, arouses interest, implants desire, and instills trust and belief.
2. Teacher reads an example of a personal ad.
3. Each child writes his/her own personal ad stressing strengths. Remind them that they are selling themselves, they are important, and they want others to feel they'd be missing something if they did not meet them. The students are NOT to put their names in the ad or on the front of the final copy of the ad.
4. After the rough draft is edited and corrected, the student rewrites it on good composition paper. The student's name goes on the back lightly in pencil.
5. Teacher assigns each paper a number randomly and quietly tells each student what his/her number is.
6. Classmates can try to guess which ad goes with which student. The student doing the guessing should state why he/she would want to meet the ad writer.

156. A strength a day

Procedures:

1. Choose a strength and write it on the board. Ask students to brainstorm about ways they could demonstrate this strength. Write them on the board.
2. Do this for other strengths (should have 5-10 ways to demonstrate each strength).
3. Have students copy notes from the board. Alternatively, teacher could provide copies of the material.
4. Students are to do one thing from the list each day. (They may choose to do the same thing every day or a different one.)
5. At the end of the week the students should write down the things they did and which strengths these actions were associated with. The students should drop their list in the Strength Box (shoe box). The teacher can then see which strengths are possessed by which students.

Materials:

Teachers list or notebooks, shoe box.

157. Quality word search

Procedures:

1. Have students list at least ten qualities that they find in themselves. They should also list five physical qualities about themselves. Arrange the words vertically, horizontally, backwards, forwards, upside down, etc., in a word search and fill in letters randomly in the empty spaces. Use graph paper for puzzle boards.

2. Make copies and distribute the puzzles to the class and let the students solve them. This activity allows students to see qualities in themselves and in others.

3. Another variation is to form teams of pairs of students who will make a word search of each other's qualities. This allows the students to see qualities in others using their own judgment. Collect and redistribute the puzzles. The students will complete the word searches and guess to whom they belong

158. Buddy biographies

Procedures:

Form pairs of students. Their task is to be an author of a biography about their partner. They conduct an interview with questions they have developed themselves. Students may also interview other people for additional information. (e.g., friends, teachers, family members.) The biography should be a story that tells about the life of the buddy, but more importantly, should discuss the strengths of this individual.

The purpose of this activity is for students to recognize their own strengths and those of their peers. Each student will benefit not only from the experience of learning about someone else, but also from hearing all the strengths others see in him/herself.

159. The name game

Procedures:

1. Arrange the students so that they are sitting in a circle, facing each other. This game may be played in the gym, in the yard or in the classroom. The game starts by having the first person stand, say his or her name, and then a one word quality they possess. Then the next person stands, repeats the first person's name and quality and then says his/her own name and quality. This

game progresses in the same fashion as the game "I went on a picnic and I brought...". In this game the students get to know each other and their special qualities. If someone cannot remember someone's name and quality when it is their turn, that person will go to the end of the circle and will get a chance to try again.

2. This game uses the skill of memory. With the constant repetition of the student's names and qualities, the students will be able to look for these and other qualities in themselves and others. Each time the game is played, have the students pick different qualities for themselves.

3. As the students are playing the game, the teacher can make a list of their names and qualities on a chart.

160. Positive and negative characteristics

Procedures:

1. Ask students to consider positive and negative characteristics of a person.

2. Each characteristic should be recorded on the number line. The positive characteristic which is *most important* to the individual would be written near a high positive number, etc.

3. Ask students to note how they compare to the picture they created.

Materials:

1. ready-made number line, including positive and negative axes, for each student.

2. Pen or pencil.

CHAPTER FOUR

Values instruction

Values may be defined as something we prize or hold dear. Kluckholm states that "A value is a conception, explicit or implicit, distinctive of an individual or characteristic of a group, of the desirable which influences the selection from available modes, means and ends of action." Values may be moral standards that guide decision-making, or the criteria by which goals and attitudes are formed. In short, values are standards of desirability by which individuals choose alternatives.

"Values instruction" is of primary importance to enhancing the self. Why? Because values are of crucial importance to the understanding of the student's functioning, especially in the area of decision-making and goal-setting. Specifically, values are motivating factors in determining goals. Therefore, when students learn to understand and accept their own values, they can set and achieve a more realistic and personally successful group of goals.

What is meant by "values instruction"? Does it imply that teachers should indoctrinate children with their own personal values? Can the teacher prepare a short list of universally accepted values to be inculcated in children? These questions are vital, for they concern the ethics of value instruction. It is precisely this ethical problem that has kept values per se out of school curriculums — though not out of classrooms. For values are being taught today — accidentally, haphazardly — by teachers who are often not even aware that they are teaching values. Any time teachers "explain" an event or situation, they do so using their own values, which are thus transmitted to the class. The average child attending American elementary and secondary schools will come into contact with at least 30 different teachers, and while this diversity may save the child from a "values brainwashing" from any one teacher, it also tends to neutralize any positive effects such exposure might offer. The child ends high school with many conflicting values — and considerable confusion.

Obviously, it is impractical to attempt to teach the child the personal values of any one teacher. But the second alternative — teaching all children the same unified values — is equally problematic. Ethically, the teacher must hesitate before launching into any large-scale values indoctrination program. While it is certainly more effective than conflicting instructions from individual teachers, this approach smacks too much of group mind control to merit serious consideration in this country. It has been said that we live in an ethicless society where people have lost their sense of values — where else but in the school system will values be taught? Still the question remains, do students really need values instruction? This concerns not only the what of values instruction but also the why. Laura Huyssen comments on this issue:

Given the complex and rapidly changing nature of our society, it appears that educators are irresponsible if not downright destructive in dealing with children if they attempt to teach children their (the teacher's or the school's) values. The world the child lives in when grown will surely be different due to social change. The particular segment of that world which makes up the person's environment as an adult may be very different from that in which he grew up, due to his own experiences or perhaps social mobility. The values of one time and sub-group may well not be values for another time or sub-group. And yet value issues are vital to human life and experience and are ignored by educators at their client's peril. It appears that in the area of values, as well as in many subject matter areas, there is a need to move toward aiding a student in acquiring not a static set of rules or facts or formulae, but a process which he can set into motion to deal with life problems. Thus, an emphasis on development of the value system and valuing process should replace an emphasis on training "good habits."

Let us propose, therefore, that what children really need is not a set of ready-made values, but rather principles, tools, and reliable information by which they may develop effective values of their own. This approach would offer the child a dynamic flexibility essential in a world of transition, while providing him with a reliable framework in which to function.

Assuming that this is what the teacher is hoping to achieve, how can we bring it about? What teacher behaviors would help the child acquire these value-forming tools? Raths, Harmin, and Simon consider this problem in their book, Values and Teaching, and suggest that teachers should:

1. Encourage children to make choices and to make them freely.

2. Help children to discover and examine the available alternatives when faced with choices.

3. Help children to weigh alternatives thoughtfully, reflecting on the consequences of each.

4. Encourage children to consider what it is that they prize and cherish.

5. Give children opportunities to make public affirmations of their choices.

6. Encourage children to act, behave, and live in accordance with their choices.

7. Help children to examine repeated behaviors or patterns in their lives.

The authors explain that these techniques will encourage the process of valuing and help children clarify for themselves what values are and what their own values are. This particular approach is a strong affirmation of humanity and human potential, implying that "...human beings hold the possibility of being thoughtful and wise and that the most appropriate values will come when persons use their intelligence freely and reflectively to define their relationships with each other and with an ever-changing world. Furthermore, it is based on the idea that values are personal things if they exist at all, that they cannot be of much significance if they do not penetrate the living of the person who holds them."

Children can develop valid, effective values if they are provided with the necessary tools. The following techniques have been developed for this purpose. These techniques are all directed toward a "values education" that teaches what values are and promotes individual development of personal values. I have faith in children. I have faith in teachers. I have faith in people. And this, basically, is what this section is all about.

Early Childhood/Elementary School

161. Fantasy wishes

Procedures:

1. Distribute a piece of paper and a pencil to each child.
2. Ask the children to write down a fantasy wish.
3. Put all of the papers into a hat.
4. Ask the children to sit on the floor and make a circle.
5. Each child will take turns randomly picking a wish out of the hat. The child will tell what value underlies the wish.

Materials:

Small pieces of paper, pencils, a hat

162. Sing a Song of Value

Procedures:

1. Play records for the class.
2. In small groups, children will react to the songs. (Who may be singing? What are they saying? Why?)

Materials:

Records containing songs about values and personal interactions.

163. Last person on earth

Procedures:

1. Ask each student what five items he/she would like to have if he/she was the last person on earth.
2. Students in small groups,may share their lists and the reasons for the choices.

164. Bar Graph of Values

Procedures:

1. Provide students with a list of values. The type and number are dependent upon level of students).
2. Ask each student to draw a bar graph using the assigned value. The height of each bar represents the importance of the corresponding value.
   It may be helpful to assign a common maximum height, e.g. the value of greatest importance would be 50 units high.
3. Share and display graphs.

Materials:

Graph paper or oak tag, pen, pencil and crayons

165. Value mobile

Procedures:

1. Distribute all of the materials mentioned below to the children.
2. The children will cut out pictures from the magazines that represent their values.
3. The children will draw pictures that represent their values if they can't find them anywhere else.
4. The children will write down adjectives that describe their values.
5. Hang all of the various values on the hanger with pieces of string.
6. Display the mobiles around the classroom.

Materials:

magazines, construction paper, glue, scissors, colored markers, wire hanger, pieces of string

166. Collages

Procedures:

1. Distribute all of the materials below to the children.
2. The children will cut out pictures of things that they like or of things that are important to them.
3. The children will glue the pictures on the construction paper in an overlapping fashion.
4. When the collages are finished, the children's values will be discussed.

Materials:

Magazines, scissors, glue, construction paper

167. Field trips

Procedures:

1. Plan several field trips to museums/homes of famous figures in history.
2. Set a purpose for each trip. The purpose should be to consider three values of the historical figure based on observations of exhibits and information provided at the site.
3. When students return to class, ask them to discuss observations in a small group and to come to an agreement among the group members.
4. One spokesperson from each group presents the three values the group believes were possessed by the historical figure. They should be presented in order of importance with evidence given for each value.

168. Picture my values

Procedures:

1. The class will have a discussion about values. What is a value?
2. Divide class into groups of five students.
3. Allow students to cut out pictures from the magazines which are representative of their values. (The pictures may represent where the value stemmed from or where it may lead you in the future). Example: For a sixth grader for whom playing baseball is of great importance, he may cut out a picture of a little child playing Little League softball [past], a picture of a bat and ball [present], or a picture of Darryl Strawberry, NY Mets outfielder [future].
4. Students paste their snapshots somewhere on the construction paper and then paste their "value" pictures around the snapshot and paper creating a collage.
5. Class discussion should follow the activity. What did you like or dislike about the activity and why? Did you discover values you did not realize you had?

Materials:

Construction paper, scissors, glue and magazines

169. Diamente poetry

Procedures:

1. Introduce the children to the format of Diamete poetry.

One word

Two adjectives

Three action verbs

Four word phrase describing word

Three action verbs

Two adjectives

One word

2. Choosing either Success, Values or Strengths, have the children write a diamente poem about themselves. Encourage the children to use the thesaurus to help them write their poems.

170. Dear Mr. President

Procedures:

1. Tell the children that they are going to write a letter to the President of the United States. Pass out lined paper.
2. Instruct them to write about things they would like the President to change and why they feel these changes are important ones.
3. They could also add anything that they feel directly relates to them. For example, "I would like you to get rid of the drug problem because on my way to school people try to sell me drugs."
4. The letters should be read aloud when the children are finished. This exercise gives the teacher a clue to the children's values.
   Optional: The teacher can mail the letters to the President.

171. Cartoon talk

Procedures:

1. Give each child four pieces of paper.
2. Ask the students to listen to a situation. Example: Susan has a Science test tomorrow and she has not studied yet. After she got home from school, Tom invited her to a party.
3. Ask the children to use one piece of paper to illustrate and to write dialogue for a five frame comic strip to continue the story. The comic strip must tell what happened and why certain choices were made.

4. This will be repeated for three more situations. (You could do this every week using different situations regarding drugs, friends, school, etc.)

5. The students would break into small groups of four and share responses. They will also discuss what value judgments and decisions were made in each comic strip.

Materials:

White drawing paper, crayons or markers, pencils

172. Skits that reveal values

Procedures:

1. Ask students to choose a profession.
2. Perform skit exemplifying profession.
3. Why do they consider profession important?
4. What is least valued about it?

Materials:

Various hats, clothes

173. Analyzing articles for values

Procedures:

1. Break up the class into groups of six.
2. Give each group a magazine article. The group will determine what values are expressed in the article.
3. Have each group present the values found in the article.

Materials:

Magazine articles dealing with values

174. Learning fractions

Procedures:

1. List values on the board.
2. Children indicate what fraction of themselves is devoted to each of the values listed on the board.

175. Aesop's fables

Procedures:

1. Read the children an Aesop fable about the *Ant* and *The Grasshopper*. Explain that these stories are older than this country, that people had listened to them before the birth of Christ, and that the stories contain wisdom.
2. Discuss the stories and the characters. Then ask the students to give examples of similar events in their own lives or act out these events, emphasizing the values operating within the experience.
3. In order to lead students to discovering what values are depicted, the teacher should ask question such as:

   - What does the grasshopper think of the ants at the beginning? Why does he laugh at them?
   - What do the ants think of the grasshopper?
   - When are you like the grasshopper? When are you like the ants?
   - Should we *always* be one way or the other? Are there times when it is good to be an "ant"? A "grasshopper"?.
   - What is the value that makes the ants work hard and save their food? What is the value that makes them share it with the grasshopper?

Materials:

A collection of Aesop's fables

176. Chef's Menu of Values

Procedures:

1. The teacher hands out to each child a menu of values. This is the menu.
   Honesty
   Education
   Good Looks
   Happiness
   Become Famous or Well Known
   Kindness
   Successful accomplishments
   Independence - Doing things on your own
   Having power over others
   Enjoyment of Art and Music
   Health

2. Each child is directed to select seven (7) of his/her personal values from this list.

3. Each child is then given a complete table setting. The table setting consists seven different items: plastic utensils, three paper plates, a paper bowl, a paper cup, and a napkin.

4. Each item will be inscribed with a a number from 1 to 7 representing a different level of the meal. Appetizer plate is #1, Soup bowl is designated as item #2, paper cup is designated as item #3, plate for main course has three different item numbers on it, #4, 5, 6. The dessert dish is designated as item #7.

5. The seven values that the child has previously selected from the menu list is written down in the order of importance.

6. Each child is told to list the least important value on the appetizer plate, the next most important value on the soup bowl, the third most important value on the paper cup, and so forth... until the table setting is completed, with the most important value written on the dessert dish.

7. The teacher now goes around to every child individually. Each child is asked to name their values in ascending order starting with the appetizer, and is asked to explain why he/she have chosen a particular value.

8. The teacher now refers back to the original menu that was distributed to the class. The list is written on he blackboard. As each child reads his/her list to the class, the teacher places the number next to the value.

9. The numbers are tallied. The children are able to see which value scores the highest number of points. At the end of the game, the class will have reached a concensus, as to what values hold the most significant meaning for the class as a whole.

10. Classroom discussion is conducted.

11. The children are given an assignment. They are asked to make up a short story, which can be fiction or non-fiction, using themselves as one of the characters. The story must include the most important values decided upon in the classroom discussion and end with a moral.

Materials:

A table setting consisting of: plastic utensils, paper plates, a paper bowl, a napkin, and a paper cup.

177. A Value Flag

Procedures:

Instruct the students to design a flag representing their personal values. They must associate a symbol with their most important value(s) and draw it (them) on a paper flag. If the value were "peace in the world", say, the symbol could be a dove.

178. Monthly "Guess Who"

Procedures:

1. Each student writes a composition describing personal values, (things that they cherish or deem important).
2. Teacher assigns a number to each composition and reads it to class without telling the author. Students listen, write the number, and write the name of the persons they believe wrote it.
3. After all compositions are read, answers are given and students check their list to see how well they know their classmates.

Materials:

writing paper

179. One Minute TV Spot

Procedures:

1. Students develop a one minute spot to be aired on TV which will promote their own personal message.
2. The class tries to determine what values underlie this TV message.

Junior High/High School

180. Just what are your values?

Procedures:

> This value centered lesson will focus on what each student will do when they are presented with a "moral dilemma" A discussion will then ensue and the teacher will act as the devil's advocate to get a debate going for each side of the issue.
>
> The topics to be assigned are not limited to the following:
>
> a) Should abortions be legalized?
> b) If you found $300 in cash and no one saw you find it, would you make an effort to find the owner"
> c) You see your best friend copying your answers on the City Wide Test. Should you tell your teacher?
> d) Are their any circumstances which merit fighting?
> e) If you saw your parents using drugs, should you tell someone?
>
> Teachers should be very careful not to inject their own views to their students. Hopefully, the teacher will try to get the students to *carefully* consider all the possibilities, and come up with their own values on these issues.

181. Talking about pictures

Procedures:

1. Ask children to bring in pictures from home. These can be pages from magazines, or photographs, or even pictures they have drawn themselves.

2. Ask the children to talk about their pictures. This will probably tell you a great deal about what the children consider to be important.

3. Have them exchange pictures and let them try to talk about one another's pictures. This way the children can learn about each other' values.

Materials:

Pictures from home or magazines

182. What would you take

Procedures:

In the summer of 1989 Hurricane Hugo hit Charleston, South Carolina destroying many homes and business. As the storm neared Charleston, television reporters were warning people of the danger of the storm. Two hours prior to the onset of the storm's major force one reporter said, "If you want to leave the area, leave now. If you wait any longer it will be too dangerous to leave." Many people left their homes wondering if they would ever see them again.

1. Break up the class into discussion groups of 4-6 students and pose the following question: If you had to evacuate your home and you could take only three things with you what would you take? You must be able to carry the three items in your arms.

2. After the students have chosen the three items, rank them in order of importance, with 1 representing the the most important.

3. They also have to explain why they chose the three items and why the ones they ranked as most important are most important.

183. New Year's Resolution

Procedures:

1. Make a list of the things you want to change about your life. Such things might include your job, your environment, etc.
2. Rank order this list according to their importance.
3. Key the list to identify the values inherent in the things you want to change.

184. Value squares

Procedures:

1. Clear out the center of the room. Then place 9 desks in a tic-tac-toe shape in the center. Nine students should then sit in those desks. They will be the stars.
2. Two contestants should be chosen. These contestants will take turns choosing a "Square".
3. The star in that square will relate to the contestant a situation they encountered and a choice they made.
4. The contestant must then identify the value involved in the choice.
5. The "Star" then tells if the contestant is correct. If correct, the contestant puts their marker on the Star's desk, X or O. The game continues until a contestant gets tic-tac-toe.

185. The model society

Procedures:

1. Discuss the three different kinds of societies in which people live. Tell the class that they are going to research the three different societies.
2. They will then pick the one that they would be the happiest living in.

3. After they have decided, they are to make a model of this environment. The model may be made out of clay, wood, paper, paper mache, wire or any material they can obtain. They may also choose to make a diorama of the society. The children may work in pairs if they wish. This project must be done over a period of time. Allow class time to work on it. Also, encourage the students to bring in materials from home that can be used in their models.

4. When the models are constructed, have each student or group of students display the model in front of the class and tell why that society was chosen.

5. Each student should attach an index card that says why they chose that society over the other ones, what kind of life they would lead and three reasons why they think this is the best society to live in and what that society has to offer.

This activity allows the children to make choices, and look at their values.

Materials:

Books on rural, urban and suburban areas, assorted craft materials (clay, colored paper, tissue paper, paint, markers, shoe boxes).

186. Parade of values

Procedures:

Discussions and other activities have already taken place for a period of two weeks. The students are aware of the strengths and the values they posses.

1. The students and the teacher have been bringing in scrap materials for this project for two weeks.

2. Briefly review and summarize the previous discussions of values.

3. The students will write at least three values they possess.

4. Instruct the students to use the materials brought to school to create a parade float depicting the three values they have written.

5. Each float must be no larger than the student desk nor smaller than a shoe box.

Materials:

scrap materials

187. Value timeline

Procedures:

1. Students will be asked to write a timeline of their life.
2. At each time interval (5 years), students are to put a picture of something that they valued at the time.
3. Timelines are to be shared with the class.
4. The purpose of this activity is for students to recognize how their values have changed as they grow older.

188. Priorities

Procedures:

1. Ask students to write what they would do as President of the United States.
2. List the responsibilities of that office in order of importance.
3. Teacher can identify student's values through the list.

Materials:

History books and books about government

189. Era student would like to have lived in

Procedures:

1. Students pick an era which interests them.
2. Explain why they chose this period.
3. Students pick historical figure from that era and read a biography of that person.
4. Students describe how they identify with that figure.

Materials:

History and biography books

190. World leaders

Procedures:

1. Have each student choose a world leader to role play.
2. They research information and locate country on map.
3. State how they would solve current conflicts in the country.
4. The student should state if they are concerned with the country's well being or world peace.

Materials:

History books, biography world map, newspaper

191. Development of values

Procedures:

1. Have students write composition on what they think their future will be like.
2. Pass compositions to other students and have them identify four most evident values.
3. Discuss with students how they think their values developed.

192. $1,000 to spend

Procedures:

1. Tell students that they will be given $100 to spend on two things.
2. Identify values in what students choose.

193. What would you die for?

Procedures:

1. Propose the hypothetical question, "What would you die for?"
2. Conduct a class discussion of this question. Students values will be revealed through their answers.

194. Societal values

Procedures:

1. Discuss why everyone is an individual in society.
2. Cite historical examples in different societies.
3. Explain why their values can have positive or negative connotations in society.
4. Discuss why different societies treat values differently.

195. Utopian society

Procedures:

1. Define "utopian".
2. Have students describe and write about their utopian society.
3. Determine their values from writing about their utopian society.

196. Presidential convention

Procedures:

1. Hold a mock Presidential campaign.
2. Students will establish a platform.
3. Students will debate campaign issues.
4. Class will discuss values evident in debate.

197. Leadership

Procedures:

1. The teacher stimulates the student's imaginations by telling them that they have just arrived in an unexplored region and have been chosen as leader of their group.
2. The teacher asks, "What ideals would you stress in directing your followers?"

198. Open ended questions

Procedures:

1. Have students complete open ended questions i.e., If I had 24 hours to live I would ... The purpose of my life is ...
2. The teacher identifies the values in these statements.
3. The class discusses these values.

Materials:

Worksheet with open-ended questions
Some other open ended questions that have proved productive:
With a gift of $100, I would ...
If this next weekend were a three-day weekend, I would want to ...
My best friend can be counted on to ...
My bluest days are ...
I can hardly wait to be able to ...

My children won't have to ... because ...
People can hurt my feelings the most by ...
If I had a car of my own ...
I've made up my mind to finally learn how to ...
If I could get a free subscription to two magazines, I would select ... because ...
Some people seem to want only to ...
The night I stayed up later than ever before I ...
If I could have seven wishes they would be ...
I believe ...
Secretly I wish ...
My advice to the world would be ...

199. Stories relating to values

Procedures:

1. Divide class into groups with similar values.
2. Each group creates a story relating to their values.
3. Each group presents it to the class and debates why their "value" story is important.

200. Planning a school

Procedures:

1. Ask students to plan a new school.
2. Ask them what would be valued in the school.

201. Comparing values

Procedures:

1. Ask students to make a list of their mother's, their father's and their own values.
2. Ask students to compare the three lists and find out what they have in common.

202. Cornerstone

Procedures:

1. Tell students to imagine that they have the privilege of putting an object in the cornerstone of a building to be opened in the future.
2. Discuss with the class what they chose and why.
3. Relate their answers to values.

203. Reincarnation rap

Procedures:

1. Define reincarnation.
2. Ask the class what they would like to be in their second life.
3. Relate their answers to values.

204. Insurance

Procedures:

1. Define an insurance policy.
2. Have students write up their own insurance policies (listing things that they value and explaining why they wouldn't want to lose them.)

205. What would I take?

Procedures:

1. Tell class they are going on a trip to the moon and will be there for several months. Each student is permitted to take three things that they value.
2. Have students list the three things and explain why each item is of value.

206. Bartering

Procedures:

1. On three separate pieces of paper, have each student write three things that are important to them that they would like to buy or sell.
2. Teacher collects them and tapes them on the board.
3. Class barters for items they want.

207. Poetry and values

Procedures:

1. Introduce poetry to students.
2. Have students re-examine their values as compared to the poets.

Materials:

Poetry which deals with values.

208. The short story and values in conflict

Procedures:

Prose fiction (and the short story in particular) is structured around conflict. A story may deal with an actual value conflict within one individual or between two values. In either case, values are central to the discussion of the story's conflict.
It is possible to consider the values in a story from three aspects.

1. Students may examine the story for the values expressed or manifested by the author or the characters.
2. The values expressed or manifested in the story may be compared to those present in other stories from the same period.
3. Students may compare the values in the story with values operative in their own lives.

209. Values in decision-making

Procedures:

1. Students describe an important decision they recently made.
2. Analyze the values that were operative in the decision.

210. Positive and negative values

Procedures:

1. Ask students to clip two news items, one that represents a value used in a positive way and one that represents a value used in a negative way.
2. Are there similarities among the positive ones?
3. Are there similarities among the negative ones?

Materials:

Newspaper

211. A play about values

Procedures:

1. Have students write and produce a play.
2. The main character must make a choice between two equally strong and important values.

212. Political speeches

Procedures:

1. Collect several speeches of candidates either from current literature or historical documents.
2. Study these speeches for consistency or conflict of values.
3. What values are expressed?

Materials:

Newspapers

213. Advertisements and values

Procedures:

1.   Students collect a series of advertisements.
2.   The advertisements must influence our social and economic values.
3.   Analyze the values emphasized in the advertisements.
4.   Can advertisements change our attitudes in ways inconsistent with our basic beliefs? Why or why not?

Materials:

Newspapers and magazines

214. Doors

Procedures:

1.   Label various doors with different values.
2.   Tell the students to choose only one.
3.   Ask what they would most like to find behind the door - related to the value, e.g. power door, be king, etc.
4.   This will show what value the student considers the most important, then have them differentiate within the value.

Materials:

Labels to put on doors

215. An author in his time

Procedures:

1.   Have students choose and do research on famous authors in relation to their social, cultural, and historical background.

2. Ask them to present a report on why they feel the authors were or were not accepted in their day. This will help students to discover for themselves how opinions are formed and how easily they can influence the acceptance or rejection of other people's values and the expression of them.

216. Changing values through history

Procedures:

1. Describe and research life in the Middle Ages.
2. Explain that both serf & feudal lordes were concerned with the salvation of the soul. They expected a short life filled with trials and tribulations.
3. Discuss our present concerns with happiness and prosperity.
4. Discuss with students why values have changed over time.

Materials:

History books

217. Changing values of government

Procedures:

1. Study changes in government services for the needy over the years (aged, unemployed, homeless, etc.)
2. How can the students see the values of government changing over the years?
3. What do the students think brought about these changes?

Materials:

History books, government publications

218. Shopping game

Procedures:

1. Give the students each and imaginary $1,000.
2. Tell them that each item costs $100.
3. Have them purchase the items most important to them.
4. Identify values through their purchases. (Make sure that the list contains at least 20 items.)

SAMPLE LIST OF VALUES

The opportunity to make your own decisions and live by them. (Autonomy)

Great looks. (Physical Attractiveness)

A chance to rid the school of unfairness and prejudice. (Humanitarianism)

An anti-hangup pill. (Emotional Well Being)

An honesty pill. (Honesty)

Lots of money. (Economic)

A chance to help students in need. (Humanitarianism)

A car of your own. (Autonomy)

A chance to see all the plays and museums in New York. (Aesthetic)

A change to be named one of the "Outstanding Students of the Year." (Recognition)

A straight A average. (Achievement)

A chance to be president of the student body. (Power)

A chance to do independent study on a subject that really interest you. (Knowledge)

A chance to do in school what you would really like to do. (Autonomy)

A chance to really appeal to members of the opposite sex. (Physical Attractiveness)

A "goodness" pill. (Humanitarianism)

Good advice and counseling from someone who really understands. (Emotional Well Being)

The love and admiration of all those who know you. (Recognition)

The ability to always know the right thing to do. (Wisdom)

A chance to be able to say what you really think and do what you want (Autonomy)

A chance to buy whatever you want for the next week. (Economic)

A chance to work to better our community and school. (Humanitarian)

A year's vacation of just fun and play. (Pleasure)

A chance to be popular and well-known in school. (Recognition)

A chance to lead one of the school teams to victory. (Power)

A chance to help make decisions concerning school policy. (Power)

A room full of books on all subjects always at your disposal. (Knowledge)

Materials:

Chart of things for sale

219. Value Flea Market

Procedures:

1. Cards are set up at various value tables.
   Examples of how the cards may be labeled are:
   Kindness, Health, Happiness, Excellent Grades, Fairness, Athletic Ability, Good Looks, Money, etc.
2. Students may select five values from the appropriate tables. In this way students choose values which are most important to them, since they are limited to choosing only five.
3. Each student then lists the purchased values on a piece of paper assigning a number indicating the priority of preference of each value.
4. Follow with a class discussion of why the values were chosen.

   (The Sample List of Values given in #218 may be helpful.)

CHAPTER FIVE

Conflict management

Conflict is the emotional tension resulting from incompatible needs, drives, goals or values either within or between individuals. It is the inevitable result of the confluence of opposing ideas, courses of action or behavior. Therefore, it is obvious that positive, constructive methods for the management of such conflict are essential to the achievement of meaningful goals.

In a classroom situation, learning conflict management is crucial. Basically, there are two essential skills involved, i.e., the elements of problem-solving and communication. If children learn to participate in problem-solving when they enter school, and continue practicing with a variety of teachers throughout their school career, they will be able to solve problems outside of school with family, friends, employers, etc. They will approach problems in a more disciplined manner. In addition, they will be responsible for their own behavior or actions and their consequences in dealing with themself and others.

Effective problem-solving on any grade level must include an analysis of the following four questions: What is the real problem to be solved? What are the choices or alternatives? What are the solutions and consequences? and How can I convert the answers to these questions into action? In answering these questions logic, insight and creativity must be kept in mind.

In order to master the art of problem-solving, students must have certain qualities. Students must be empathic listeners which means that they must analyze and understand the meaning behind human behavior. It is a deflating and lonely experience when students feel that others are not listening. But when others are listening, their egos are enhanced and they feel understood and cared about. In addition, students must have an attitude of openness and flexibility when listening to others. The aims of the following techniques are for students to become in touch with their feelings, to enhance their ability to communicate and to allow them to be diverse in their methods of problem-solving.

The end result in problem-solving is that the students are not "boxed in" by using one method. They learn to use diverse methods to make the right and practical decision that is compatible with themself and people they deal with.

Early Childhood/Elementary School

220. Decision-making

Procedures:

1. Tell the class they are given $500 as a gift.
2. They can decide to buy anything they want.
3. The whole class must agree on the item.
4. If one person disagrees they must either convince that person to go along or decide on another item.

221. Token system

Procedures:

1. The token system must be fully explained to children before beginning it.
2. Each child is given a token (color-coded) for positive behavior immediately after the desired behavior appears.
3. Positive tokens earn children a reward which is meaningful to them (cash in tokens for trips).
4. When behavior improves, children earn more positive tokens.
5. If the rewards are meaningful the child will modify behavior to earn rewards.

Materials:

Different colored chips

222. Unfinished story

Procedures:

1. Tell the children a story in which the characters are in conflict - stop at the conflict.
2. The children must decide on a solution.
3. Have them discuss their ideas.
4. Act as a reflective listener while students give their solutions.

223. Fantasy

Procedures:

1. Use Gestalt technique of multifaceted personality - i.e., there are two people inside your head - one saying you should do something (steal, cut school, etc.) and the other saying you shouldn't.
2. The students act out both parts and have a discussion between the two people - decide who wins.

224. Punching bag technique

Procedures:

It is important to help the children to recognize situations that are "explosive" for them, to become aware of their responses, and to explore possible alternatives for handling such situations. The following technique would be most advantageous in special education classes or in groups of young people who have difficulty handling aggression in conflict situations.

1. Create an environment in which the expression of feelings is acceptable. If two children become involved in an explosive situation and there is a high probability that physical violence will result, allow the children to fully vent their anger on a punching bag or to retire to the quiet corner.
2. If the child is willing to verbalize his anger while punching the bag or sitting in the quiet corner, the tape recorder should be used and the child should listen to the playback. This is an invaluable opportunity to listen and to hear oneself. Then, if they are able, both children should be allowed to discuss the incident.
3. The teacher's role should be one of channeling energies into less destructive modes, recognizing the anger, and helping children to discover their patterns that cause loss of control. These patterns can become evident to children when they hear themselves in these situations. After recognition of the patterns, the child should find the means

to avoid or handle these situations. The teacher should be available as a resource for exploration through reflective listening. The quiet corner can serve as a place where a child might withdraw from an explosive situation. While he/she is using it, no one else may disturb him/her until either one chooses to return to the group.

4. Each time children avoid or handle situations in a socially acceptable manner, they should be highly praised and rewarded for their success.

Materials:

Punching bag

225. Breaking out of a circle

Procedures:

1. Ask younger children to join hands and form a circle.
2. One stays in the middle and that person's job is to try to break out of the circle while the students forming the circle are to keep he/she inside.
3. When the game is over, those who had to keep their peer inside should discuss how they felt about excluding one member, specifically what they did, and which techniques they thought were successful.
4. The child in the center should talk about his/her feelings and what he/she tried to do to get free.
5. Children are engaging in a physical activity that could relieve tension, and they are understanding and examining their own feelings. The game should be played several times so that many children have the chance to play each of the roles.

226. Dear Abby

Procedures:

1. The student should write a letter asking for advice in the form of a Dear Abby or Ann Landers letter. Read a sample letter from the newspaper to the class.
2. Students should be asked to respond to a letter from one of their classmates giving the advice asked for.
3. Set aside time to read, discuss and try to solve the problem(s).

227. "What's Bugging Me Box"

Procedures:

1. Have children decorate a cardboard box with construction paper and markers.
2. Make sure they leave an opening on the top of the box (like a ballot box) large enough to be able to slip a piece of paper.
3. They may want to draw insects and bugs on the box. Label it the "What's Bugging Me Box".
4. Explain that the purpose of the box is to be able to anonymously place a piece of paper in the box containing a problem that the student may be facing. The problem can be academic, social, home related or any other facet of their lives.
5. The author of the note will be anonymous.
6. At the end of each week the box will be emptied and the whole class will try to offer solutions and various alternatives on how to handle, solve or deal with these problems.

Materials:

Cardboard box, construction paper, markers

228. I appreciate

Procedures:

> When two children get into a disagreement over something, use this classroom procedure to help them learn that you can always appreciate something about a person. Break off further discussion of the problem until each child has come up with an ending to this statement; I appreciate . . . . because he/she
> This will help children to appreciate the strengths in other people.

229. April Rain

Procedures:

1. Place large construction paper umbrella on the bulletin board.
2. Have children brainstorm about problems in the classroom (or note problems that occur in classroom). For example: not enough blocks, no room on the circle, children call out, etc.
3. Write these problems on large gray construction paper "raindrops." Try to have one for each child. Scatter the "raindrops" on the bulletin board.
4. Cut out an equal number of sunshines with each child's name on a sun.
5. During the month any child who solves a problem (shares, makes room for others, etc.) can replace that raindrop with a sun bearing the child's name.

230. Practice problems

Procedures:

1. Simulate problem situations.
2. Follow a problem solving method of defining the problem, generating solutions, evaluating and selecting solutions, and devising a plan of action. Sample problems:

a. Porky Pig went out for a long walk and when he came back, his favorite watering hole had dried up.

b. The class planned an outdoor picnic and it is pouring rain outside

231. Check system

Procedures:

1. Have each child's name written on the blackboard.
2. Every time you "catch" that child doing something good whether it be behavior or class work, verbally acknowledge him and say, "Johnny, I like the way you are working quietly."
3. Then put a check next to his name.
4. At the end of the week these students with the most checks get to choose which monitor job they'd like for the week.
5. In addition keep track of the number of checks they get each week and at the end of the month take 4 children out to lunch for their reward.

232. Gripe sessions

Procedures:

1. Build in time to vent and discuss "Gripes" about school/others.
2. Use a "Gripe Graffiti Board" for children to write/draw gripes - then discuss.

Materials:

Colored paper, paint or crayons/markers

Junior High/High School

233. On being angry

Procedures:

1. Ask students to recall a time when they became very angry and write a short composition about it.
2. Have them try to answer as many of the following questions as they can.
   a. What specifically made you angry? What else did you feel besides anger?
   b. How important was the situation to you? Why?
   c. Were you angry at yourself, too? Why?
   d. How did you show your anger?
   e. What was the other person's reaction? How do you think he/she felt?
   f. Now that you know how the conflict ended, how would you deal with it again if it came up?
3. This may help students examine feelings they might not have been aware of and see the situation more clearly.
4. Awareness of own and others' feelings is necessary for problem solving.

234. Conflict-resolution debate

Procedures:

1. Present an issue that the class and teacher are in disagreement about (dress code, etc.)
2. Divide the class into two groups.
3. Each side takes one side of the issue and debates it.
4. See how the conflict is resolved among students.

235. Acting out the other guy's part

Procedures:

1. Take two students who are involved in a conflict?
2. Have them discuss the issue from the others' point of view so they can see the opposition's side.

236. Class court

Procedures:

1. Set up classroom rules.
2. Select a jury.
3. Those who break rules go before the jury to be judged.
4. They can also study the workings of a real court system.

237. Argument/debate

Procedures:

1. Have students listen to arguments.
2. Students will choose which sides they would take in each argument.
3. Then debate for the side they chose.
4. When they have made their point the teacher acts as an arbitrator.
5. Both sides need to debate solutions and agree on one.

Materials:

Recording of people having arguments.

238. Conflicts from literature

Procedures:

1. Choose a conflict and then have two students act it out.

2. Divide the class into two sides with all the members of each side holding the same position in the conflict. Each side formulates the reason(s) for the conflict.

3. Each side gives a set of resolutions to the conflict.

Materials:

Book or play with conflict between two or more characters.

239. Class psychologists to the rescue

Procedures:

1. Everyone plays the role of a trained psychologist.
2. The patient is a famous novel character in conflict (played by student).
3. Student tells about the conflict and how it occurred.
4. Together they discuss various solutions to the conflict, exploring all possibilities.
5. Examine how the character copes with the conflict in the novel.

Materials:

Book with characters in conflict.

240. Mock Senate

Procedures:

1. Have a presentation by several students about various bills that will benefit the class.
2. Factions will develop concerning the benefits of different bills, the priority of the bills, the usefulness of each bill to majority interests, etc.
3. A review committee (appointed or elected) will resolve any conflict of interests.

241. War conflicts

Procedures:

1. Study one war and the conflicts that were involved in starting it.
2. Have groups of students choose one country from the war and examine the way (active or passive) they dealt with the conflict.

Materials:

History books

242. Reliving history

Procedures:

1. Study a conflict in history and the viewpoints of each side taken.
2. Divide the class in half.
3. Each side will be a country and will decide on issues on which they might be able to compromise.
4. Get both sides together and see if the conflict can be solved.

Materials:

History books

243. Telephone

Procedures:

1. Present a conflict situation to the class.
2. Have them line up next to each other - the same as to play the game telephone.
3. The first person whispers a solution into the second's ear.

4. The person is allowed to change or stick to the solution and whisper their view to the next person.
5. This goes on until everyone has a turn.
6. The last person says the solution aloud.
7. Students can discuss the implications of how and why the final version differs from the original solution.

244. Conflict grab bag

Procedures:

1. Students describe a conflict they have had on a piece of paper
2. Put all the papers in a bag, mix, and let each student pick one.
3. Each student will pretend to be the person who is having conflict just selected at random.
4. Have the student explain how the conflict might be resolved.

Materials:

Paper bag

245. We've got a conflict

Procedures:

1. Present a conflict to one or two students (boys or girls).
2. Conflict: A student wants to go back to college. His/her father who needs financial security wants the students to work in the family business.
3. The students (couple) explain their conflict to the class.

246. Daily problem

Procedures:

1. Teacher writes "Problem of the Day" on board.
2. Each student can write underneath how he/she would resolve it.
3. Class discusses these ideas and tries to formulate more solutions.

247. Qualities necessary or harmful in problem-solving

Procedures:

1. Put different positive qualities necessary for problem-solving on several pieces of paper
2. Do the same for qualities which inhibit problem-solving.
3. Mix them in a hat and have each student take a paper.
4. The students pick a quality out of the hat and uses it in a problem situation.
5. The 'actors' let the class present solutions to the problem.

248. Different endings to plays

Procedures:

1. Give students a play and have them read it.
2. Discuss the ending.
3. See if they have alternate ways to end the play.
4. Discuss te reasons for the ending.

Materials:

Plays

249. Music that represents conflict

Procedures:

1. Teacher plays music that represents some kind of conflict.
2. The students express what they hear in a class discussion or in a written composition.
3. The students works are passed around the room so others can see.
4. The students are told the story behind the music.

Materials:

Record player, records

250. Fighting pairs

Procedures:

1. Class thinks of examples of fighting pairs (coyote and road runner).
2. The teacher explains that these conflicts end in physical fights.
3. Students think of solutions for handling these conflicts.
4. Students demonstrate solutions by acting them out.

251. Predetermined conclusions

Procedures:

1. Instead of asking students to search for a conclusion to a problem, give a conclusion and ask them to determine whether this conclusion is appropriate to the problem. The predetermined conclusion must be a logical one.
2. Students must work out and discuss the issues and give supporting evidence to show why the given conclusion is appropriate or inappropriate.

252. Conflict in current events

Procedures:

1. Students identify a conflict in current news.
2. Have them identify both sides of the conflict and role play each position.
3. Try to come up with a solution that will be agreeable to both sides.

Materials:

Newspapers, magazines

253. Conflict management

Procedures:

1. Students should have previous practice and know the methods of problem solving (insight, withdrawal, indifference, compromise, third-party mediation, win-lose struggles, creative problem solving.
2. Present the student with a conflict.
3. The students decide on a method of problem solving.
4. The student must use this method to solve the given conflict.

254. "What's my style"

Procedures:

1. Students tell a conflict to the class and how it was solved.
2. Students discuss whether the person solved the problem in an active or passive manner.
3. Alternatives to this style of behavior should be discussed.

Two stories for reading or class participation

Teacher's Guide

Today we're going to talk about values, and then we're going to read a story and talk about the values in it. Before we even start, though, let's figure out what a value is. A value is defined as what is important or cherished. Now, usually, when you decide to do something, you have a reason for doing it. You draw a picture, for example. You might do that for many reasons. What might some of those reasons be?

1. I like pretty things. (Aesthetic)

2. It's fun. (Pleasure)

3. My mother is proud of me when I draw nice pictures. (Recognition)

4. I want to excel in school. (Achievement)

5. I am my own boss I draw what I want to. (Autonomy)

6. I could win a dollar in a contest. (Economic)

So, people do things for different reasons. Sometimes, people have a reason to do something and another reason not to do it. Maybe I want to sit down and draw a picture, but if I do, I'll be late for school. I have a reason to do it, and a reason not to do it. How do I choose between the two? How do I choose between drawing the picture or getting to school on time?

Well, what helps you to choose is values. Values are your priorities. A value might be, "It's more important to do what I have to do (go to school) than to do what I want to do (draw the picture)," or, it might be, "It's more important to have fun," or "It's wrong to take other people's things."

Sticks and Stones May Break My Bones

A story to teach values such as respect, kindness, achievement.

After the class understands the basic definition of a value, explain what a rhyme is, if this would help children understand the story (for example, a very slow class or young children).

"Today we are going to listen to a story about a little boy who likes to make up rhymes. A rhyme is a very special way of saying something. Suppose your name was Joe, and your lawn needed to be cut. If your father said, 'Joe, go mow!' it would be a rhyme, because the words sound alike. Words that sound alike 'rhyme.' You can have a longer rhyme. You've all heard 'Roses are red, violets are blue, sugar is sweet and so are you.' This is a rhyme too, because 'blue' and 'you' sound alike or rhyme.

"The little boy in the story we're going to listen to likes to make up rhymes. But sometimes he gets in trouble because of his rhymes. Listen to the story and see if you can guess why."

Sticks and Stones May Break My Bones . . .

By Elissa Schroeder

NARRATOR: Becky and Drew were friends. Usually, they would meet after school and walk home together — but not today . . .

SOUND: Music bridge, school hall noises.

BECKY: I wonder where Drew is? He's never this late. I (softly, thinking) hope I didn't miss him — oh! There he is!

BECKY: Hi Drew! Hey, you're late. What happened, huh?
(louder)

DREW: Nothin'.
(angrily)

BECKY:	Did you have to stay after?
DREW:	I didn't do the stupid arithmetic homework.
BECKY:	Was the teacher mad?
DREW:	Yeah.
	Today's a bad day A make-you-sad day A make-you-mad day Ugly drab day!
BECKY:	Hey! We talked about rhymes in school today. And I knew what a rhyme was. I told the whole class, I have a friend who makes rhymes all the time.
DREW:	Big deal.
SOUND:	Street noises, then playground noises.
DREW:	Look at that Tony on the bar there. He can't do anything. Hey watch me, Becky. Hey! Hey Tony! Bet you can't do ten chin-ups!
SOUND:	Grunts between numbers below.
DREW:	One. Two. Three. Four. Five. Six. Seven. Eight. Nine. Ten.
TONY:	You — you look silly. You look like a stupid jumping jack. I wouldn't want to look so silly.
DREW:	You just say that because you can't do it.
TONY:	I can so too. You watch. One. Two. Three. Oh!
SOUND:	Grunts between numbers, then falling noise.
TONY:	Oh! I hurt my hand!
DREW:	See? You can't do ten, you couldn't even do four.
TONY:	Well, at least I did the arithmetic. I'm not in trouble at school. I'm not stupid- -
DREW:	Who's stupid? I'll show you- -
SOUND:	Fall.

134

TONY:	Hah! Tripped over your own stupid feet. You can't even walk.
DREW:	You-you-hey kids. Listen. I've got a new rhyme: Tony the Rat Is big and fat And more than that He's a real live brat!
SOUND:	Group of kids laughing.
KIDS:	Tony the rat! Tony the rat is big and fat! Tony the rat! That's his new name. Hey, Tony the rat!
DREW:	Look at him run. Is he mad!
BECKY:	He's crying. You made him cry.
DREW:	He's just a big cry-baby anyhow. And he said that I was stupid. I'm smarter than he is.
SOUND:	Street noises, louder.
BECKY:	Hey Drew. That's a red light. You shouldn't- -
SOUND:	Car screeching on brakes.
BECKY:	Drew! Are you all right?
DREW:	Yeah. I'm all right. But that guy . . . he was going too fast. That guy thinks he's something great Just like ice-cream on a plate And everyone can hardly wait To see him trip on a roller skate!
BECKY:	You shouldn't have crossed against the light, though. Let's go home, huh?
DREW:	I don't want to go home now. Let's go up and see Mrs. Tweezes.
BECKY:	Ok.
SOUND:	Elevator noises.
BECKY:	Boy, you really are in a bad mood. I've never seen you be so mean to people.

DREW:	I'm not being mean.
BECKY:	Yes you are. You were mean to Tony and you started a fight with him. You made all the kids laugh at him.
DREW:	You're the one who's really mean- Always try to get between Me and what I want to do- Becky Winston, who needs you?
BECKY:	That's not fair. I didn't yell.
SOUND:	Out of elevator, walking noises.
BECKY:	I wonder if she's home . . .
SOUND:	Knocking, door opening.
MRS. TWEEZES:	Why Drew! Becky! Come on in. How are you?
DREW:	Fine.
BECKY:	Fine.
MRS. TWEEZES:	Well, you don't look fine, either of you. What's the matter?
DREW:	Nothing.
BECKY:	Just a bad day.
MRS. TWEEZES:	I see. Would some chocolate mile and cookies help any?
BECKY:	Thank you, Mrs. Tweezes. That would be nice.
MRS. TWEEZES:	Uh-how was school today?
BECKY:	We — oh, we talked about rhymes.
MRS. TWEEZES:	That must have been nice.
BECKY:	I hate rhymes. Rhymes hurt people.
MRS. TWEEZES:	Oh dear. Why do you say that?

DREW:	Becky's mad with me. I made up some rhymes against people who were mean to me and she's on their side.
BECKY:	I'm not on their side.
MRS. TWEEZES:	You're good at making up rhymes, Drew. But they've always been nice ones. Were they nice ones today?
DREW:	Well, not really . . .
BECKY:	He said Tony was a fat rat . . . and all the kids laughed at him. Then he said I was mean.
MRS. TWEEZES:	Oh, that doesn't sound like you. Had Tony been mean to you?
DREW:	He said I was stupid because I had to stay after school. He laughed at me.
MRS. TWEEZES:	Oh no. That hurts, when people laugh at you.
DREW:	It made me mad.
MRS. TWEEZES:	He shouldn't have done that. People fight some-times — it just happens. But it's not right to make fun of people.
DREW:	You mean me. You're saying "Tony" but you mean me, Drew.
MRS. TWEEZES:	Well, it's true for everybody. It hurts everybody to be laughed at.
DREW:	You don't want me to make up any more rhymes.
MRS. TWEEZES:	Oh no, Drew. Why you're good at making up rhymes. It's important to be good at things.
BECKY:	Like making cookies! These taste just like real peanut butter.
MRS. TWEEZES:	Well, I'm glad you like them. Try the chocolate chip ones. No-sometimes why you do something is as important as what you do. Making rhymes is a good thing. But if your reason for doing it is bad, then it's a bad thing to do.

DREW:	But I was mad with Tony. He was mean to me. Now he knows how it feels.
MRS. TWEEZES:	Mmmmmm. I know what you mean, Drew. But you were meaner back to him that he was to you. He laughed at you — that was just one person laughing. But you made everybody laugh at him. That hurts worse.
BECKY:	But Mrs. Tweezes — isn't that like when your mother spanks you? Maybe next time Tony will know better than to laugh at Drew.
DREW:	Yeah. He won't try that again.
MRS. TWEEZES:	Well, sometimes you have to learn something and that's the only way you can learn it. Like when you grow up, Becky, and you have a baby, and maybe the baby will want to play with a knife. The baby's too little to understand why he can't play with a knife, so you might have to spank him so that he learns not to do it again. But teaching people that way is dangerous. Let me pour you some more milk.
SOUND:	Pouring.
BECKY:	Thank you.
MRS. TWEEZES:	"Teaching people a lesson" is dangerous — because people can learn the wrong thing. Like, suppose what Tony really learned today is that nobody likes him. Suppose he grew up and all his life he thought that nobody liked him. He'd have learned the wrong lesson and he'd be unhappy all his life, and for a reason that isn't true.
BECKY:	That would be awful.
DREW:	You don't think Tony really thinks that, do you? You know, that everybody hates him?
MRS. TWEEZES:	I don't know, Drew. But if he did get that idea, maybe it would be good to tell him it isn't true.

DREW: Yeah. I didn't mean to make him sad. I just wanted to get even. Maybe we could go and talk to him.

BECKY: That'd be nice. Can we take him a cookie? They're so good—

MRS. TWEEZES: Sure. And then take two for you and Drew.

BECKY: And then take two
For you and Drew.
That's a rhyme, Mrs. Tweezes! You made a rhyme too!

DREW: You make good poems and good cookies — and everything!
Mrs. Tweezes
Fast as sneezes
Nice as breezes
Always pleases!

SOUND: Ending music.

After reading the story to the class, the teacher might then ask the following or similar questions:

1. What did Mrs. Tweezes think about Drew's rhymes? Did she like the rhyme against Tony? Did she like the rhyme Drew made up about her at the end?

2. Were some of the rhymes nicer than others?

3. Why were some rhymes nice and some not so nice? (Elicit response: the rhymes that hurt people weren't nice.)

4. Do you think Drew was a mean boy or do you think he was just in a bad mood? Why was Drew unhappy?

5. Drew felt bad, so he tried to make other people feel bad too. Was this nice?

6. Mrs. Tweezes said, "It's important to be good at things." Do you think she was right? Why?

7. Mrs. Tweezes told Drew that it wasn't nice to hurt people. But Drew didn't hit Tony. Can you hurt someone by saying something? Have you ever seen that happen?

8. There's a saying, "Sticks and stones may break my bones but names will never hurt me." That's a rhyme, because stones and bones sound alike, or rhyme. Do you think that rhyme is true?

A Parrot's Not A Grizzly Bear

A story to teach values such as power, justice and kindness.

A value helps you decide between things you want. Often you can guess what a person's values are from watching the way he acts. We're going to read a story now called "A Parrot's Not a Grizzly Bear," and I'd like you to try to guess as we go along why the people in the story are acting the way they do. I'd like you to guess what their values are, by carefully watching the things they're doing.

A Parrot's Not a Grizzly Bear

By Elissa Schroeder

Summer mornings are special. You wake up and you hear your mother making noises with the frying pan. You know that pretty soon you'll be smelling bacon. You hear your father swooshing shaving cream and you know that pretty soon he'll look like Santa Claus, with a funny white shaving-cream beard. You listen to all the morning noises and you know it's time to start a new day. But it's summer. You can take your time. You don't have to hurry and get ready for school. You can wait and listen and hear the day starting.

Becky loved summer mornings. She liked to wait in bed and listen and play a game with the noises. "What are they doing now?" But not today. Today she got up right away and dressed herself as quickly as she could.

"Why Becky! You're a real early bird this morning," her mother said, putting the bacon into the hot frying pan. "Is today a special day?"

"Oh yes," Becky said, tasting her orange juice. "Today Mrs. Tweezes is going to take us to a museum."

"A museum?" her father asked, as he sat down at the table. "A museum where you see mummies and tepees and things?"

"Oh, no. This is a machine museum. There's a machine that plays tic-tac-toe with you. And a machine that hatches baby chicks just like a hen and — oh, lots of good things. Chad's class went there a long time ago and he says it's really nice."

"Well, then, you'll need a good breakfast," her mother said smiling. Becky nodded and started eating quickly. "A good slow breakfast," her father laughed. "And be sure to wash the egg off your face!"

She ate her breakfast and washed and twenty minutes later she was in the elevator on her way down to the fifth floor where Chad lived. Chad hopped in at 5 and pushed the button marked 3, for Mrs. Tweezes' floor.

"Do you think she'll really bring Milton?" Becky asked.

No. She was only joking," Chad said. "They don't let you take parrots into museums. I've been there. I know."

"Did you play the tic-tac-toe machine?"

"Sure. I almost won. It—." Just then the doors opened and they rushed down the hall to 317, where Mrs. Tweezes lived. Chad pressed the buzzer and they waited impatiently. Becky hopped from one foot to another. "You don't think she forgot, do you?"

"Of course not," Chad said, pressing the buzzer again. "Mrs. Tweezes always keeps her promises."

Just then the door opened and Mrs. Tweezes was standing there looking puzzled. "Good morning," she said slowly. "How are you today?"

"We're fine, Mrs. Tweezes. And you?" Chad asked politely.

"I'm fine — I guess. I'm just — oh, the museum! I didn't forget, children. I've been getting ready, really," she began, closing the door behind them and pointing to her half-loaded shopping bag. "I just stopped down to get my mail and—"

"We're still going, aren't we?" Becky began, but Chad nudged her.

"No bad news, I hope," he said.

"No-well-yes. I got an eviction notice."

"Is that a letter" Becky asked.

"Sort of. It's from the landlord, Mr. Bradley, and it means I have to move."

"Oh no!" both children cried together.

"Me too! Me too!" screamed Milton the parrot.

"You too is right," Mrs. Tweezes said sadly to the parrot. "You, Milton, are the whole problem."

"Milton?" Becky asked. "How is Milton the problem?"

"Mr. Bradley says that animals can't live in the building and that if I don't send Milton away, I'll have to leave the building."

"Send him away? But where?" Chad asked.

"Nowhere! Milton has been with me since he was a baby bird-and he's older than either of you. He's my family. I can't just send him away. You live with an animal this long and you-well, you love him."

"Me too! Me too!" cried the parrot.

"That's mean," Becky said angrily. "It's just not fair."

"It's his building, I guess," Mrs. Tweezes said sadly. "But I've lived here for ten years. I don't know where to go . . ."

"Maybe if you could talk to him" Chad began, "then he'd let you keep Milton. He let you keep him up 'til now; maybe he'd change his mind."

"No, I don't think so. His father used to be the landlord and he liked Milton. But now he's retired and moved away."

"But if we talked to him . . ." Becky began again.

"It's the law, Becky. He can do whatever he wants to with his property." Chad explained. "My dad told me. He's a policeman so he knows all the laws. He—" All of a sudden Chad got excited. "Hey! Wait a minute. Maybe there's another law. If there's a law for Mr. Bradley, maybe there's another law for Mrs. Tweezes."

"That would be nice, Chad, but I don't think so," Mrs. Tweezes said sadly.

"But there might be. I can ask my dad. He's home today. Let's ask him, huh?"

"If you want to, Chad - but . . ."

"Sure! Can I call on your phone? It's his day off. I know he'll come."

"All right, Chad. You know where the phone is."

Chad hurried away and Mrs. Tweezes sat down on the couch. "You children have been so good to me. Everyone in this building has been so good to me. I don't want to leave."

Becky touched her hand. "Don't cry, Mrs. Tweezes. We love you. We won't let that mean old Mr. Bradley make you leave. You're — you're like part of our families, just like Milton's part of yours. We won't let them."

"If the law says so, Becky, then that's how it has to be. People can't break laws."

Just then Chad came back. "I talked to my dad and he's coming right down."

"Oh dear - and on his day off! He loves you a lot, Chad." Mrs. Tweezes smiled, and then jumped up. "Oh, I didn't wash my breakfast dishes!"

"That's all right, Mrs. Tweezes. We'll help you. We'll dry." And they all hurried out into the kitchen and just as the last dish was finished, the doorbell rang and it was Chad's father.

144

Mrs. Tweezes let him in and Becky noticed that he wasn't wearing his policeman's uniform. It was strange to see him wearing regular clothes just like other fathers.

"Hello, Mrs. Tweezes. My boy tells me you've got some trouble." Mr. Carlson was a very big man. When he stood next to Mrs. Tweezes, she looked quite tiny.

"It's Milton, my parrot," she said. "Mr. Bradley says I'll have to send him away, or leave the building."

"Oh no!" Mr. Carlson said. "This building wouldn't be the same without you. What exactly did he say in the letter?"

"I'll show you." And she hurried to the desk and brought him back the letter. He read it silently, then frowned.

"Looks pretty bad. It seems that your lease ends this month and he wants to change it so you can't have a pet."

"What's a lease, Mr. Carlson?" Becky asked.

"Well, it's a promise, sort of. A contract, they call it. Mr. Bradley promises to let Mrs. Tweezes live here for a year, and Mrs. Tweezes promises that she'll pay him his money every month. That's rent."

"But Dad! What does that have to do with Milton?"

"Well, Chad, suppose I wanted to have a grizzly bear in our apartment. The bear might break things — and then Mr. Bradley couldn't rent our apartment ever again. He'd lose money; this apartment building is his business, just like the pet store is Becky's father's business. Or maybe Becky's family would be worried about our bear, that maybe it would hurt her. They'd move, and maybe all the other people here in the building would move and no one would want to live here. Then Mr. Bradley couldn't earn money to buy things for his kids," Mr. Carlson said, touching Chad's shoulder. "So - in this contract, he makes people promise not to have pets."

"But a parrot couldn't hurt anyone. Parrots are good." Chad objected.

"Me too! Me too!" said Milton.

"Yes, you too," Mr. Carlson laughed. "Maybe we could talk to Mr. Bradley. Maybe he'd let you stay."

"Could we? Would you come with us? You're a policeman. Then he'd have to let them stay." Becky said quickly.

"Oh no, Becky. It's not like that at all. Even a policeman can't break the law. But I'd be glad to go with you — just as another person who lives in the building. I can tell him how much all the people like Mrs. Tweezes. Maybe that would change his mind."

Oh good! Can we go now? Right away?" Becky and Chad asked together.

If Mrs. Tweezes wants to."

"Oh yes," Mrs. Tweezes said. "Do you think I should bring Milton, Mr. Carlson? Maybe if he saw that Milton is old and couldn't do anything . . ."

"Older parrots are like older people, Mrs. Tweezes. They can do a lot of good," Mr. Carlson smiled. "Let me carry his cage for you."

So they all moved out into the hall and pushed the button for the elevator.

"Do you really think he might change his mind?" Mrs. Tweezes asked. "I would hate to have to move."

"Me too! Me too!" Milton said.

"At least we will have tried," Chad's father said, holding open the elevator door.

Mr. Bradley's office was on the first floor. His secretary looked up when they all marched in. "Oh my! What a parade! Do you all live here?"

"Yes - and we all want to stay," Becky began, but Chad nudged her.

"Good morning, miss. My name is Bill Carlson, apartment 506, and this is my son Chad, and his friend Becky Winston, apartment 883. We came down to talk to Mr. Bradley about our friend Mrs. Tweezes and her parrot Milton."

"We're in apartment 317," Mrs. Tweezes added.

"I see," Mr. Bradley's secretary said. "My name is Miss Schumacher and I'll tell Mr. Bradley you're here. I know he's very busy this morning . . ."

"Me too! Me too!" Milton told her.

"Milton! Sshh!" Mrs. Tweezes said quickly, and the children laughed.

Miss Schumacher laughed too. "I guess you are! Why don't you sit down and I'll tell Mr. Bradley you're here?" She turned and went into another office.

"Oh Milton," Mrs. Tweezes said, "Please be quiet. If you make him mad, we'll have to leave." Then the door opened and Miss Schumacher came back. "Mr. Bradley will see you now."

Becky and Chad looked at each other and were scared. Would Mrs. Tweezes have to leave the building? Mr. Carlson looked down and smiled.

"Where's your courage? Sometimes you have to do things that scare you, so that you can straighten things out." And then they went in.

"Good morning," Mr. Bradley said briskly. "What seems to be the trouble?"

Mr. Carlson, said, "Well, we're here to talk to you about Mrs. Tweezes and her parrot. Does she live in the building?"

"Yes, She —"

"Well, then the parrot will have to go. No animals. That's going into all the leases now."

"But he wouldn't hurt anyone," Chad said quickly, "and she loves him - and we all love her."

"That's really true, Mr. Bradley," Mr. Carlson said. "Mrs. Tweezes is a friend to everyone in the building. The children, the adults, everyone. She's a fine lady . . . and she makes the building a nice place to live."

"That's all very well. She can stay. But the parrot has to go."

"But he's her family!" Becky said. "People can't give away their families."

"I can understand that, Becky, but a rule's a rule. Many people here don't want animals in the building. Their rights have to be respected."

"Me too! Me too!" the parrot said, and Mrs. Tweezes looked down.

""Sshh!"

"Becky, the people in this building have a right to decide what kind of a building they want to live in and if that . . ."

"Me too! Me too!"

And then Mr. Bradley stopped talking and stared at the parrot. Becky and Chad both held their breath and looked at Mr. Carlson, who seemed to be holding his breath too.

And then all of a sudden Mr. Bradley started to laugh. "This parrot of yours is a lawyer! He's arguing his own case!" And then he turned and smiled at them. "Tell him to stop arguing. He's won his case. He and Mrs. Tweezes can both stay here."

"We really appreciate that," Mr. Carlson said.

"Thank you! Thank you!" Chad and Becky cried, jumping up and down with happiness.

"Oh, I can stay. I can really stay!" Mrs. Tweezes called. "I'm so happy!"

"Me too! Me too!" cried Milton.

And everybody laughed.

OK. Now, before we read the story, we were talking about values. I asked you to watch what people did in the story so that you could guess what their values might be. You remember that we said that a value was something that helped you make a decision. What decisions did people have to make in the story? What was the story about?

Let children discuss the decisions made and the values they indicate. If the following decisions and values are not suggested, you might ask the questions listed below.

1. Becky and Chad were all set to go to the museum; they were really looking forward to it. But they didn't go. Why not? They found out that Mrs. Tweezes was in trouble. They decided not to go to the museum, but to stay and try to help her. They decided it was more important to help their friend than to have a nice trip. They said that helping people is important. This is a value.

2. What decision did Mrs. Tweezes have to make? She could either stay in the building and give away her parrot Milton or she could keep Milton and leave the building. She decided that she and Milton would stay together, because she loved him. She said that love is important. This is a value too.

3. Becky told Mrs. Tweezes that they wouldn't let Mr. Bradley send her and Milton away, but Mrs. Tweezes said, "If the law says so, then that's how it has to be." Why did she say this? What did she mean/ Mrs. Tweezes is telling Becky that the law is important. Now,

you remember that we said a value was like your very own rule for something. Well, a law is a shared value. That means that many people have the same value, or private rule. They all say "Stealing money is wrong," and it becomes a law. When Mrs. Tweezes says that she obeys the law, she means that she respects other people's values. It is important to respect other people.

4. Mr. Bradley is able to make a rule about the building, a rule that makes Mrs. Tweezes unhappy. But Chad's father says that Mr. Bradley should be able to make rules about the building. Why does he say this? Mr. Carlson, Chad's father, tells the children that if there were no rule, maybe someone would want to keep a grizzly bear in the apartment, and ruin it. Mr. Carlson says it wouldn't be fair for someone to destroy the building that way. He says fairness is important. Fairness is also called justice. When you pledge allegiance to the flag, you say "one nation . . . with liberty and justice for all." Our country says that fairness is important.

5. Why does Mr. Carlson say, "Where's your courage? Sometimes you have to do things that scare you, so that you can straighten things out." He's saying that courage is important.

6. Why does the parrot keep saying "Me too! Me too!" in Mr. Bradley's office? Mr. Bradley is talking about rights. He's saying that the other people in the building have a right not to have to live in a building with animals. But Milton says, "Me too!" because he has rights and so does Mrs. Tweezes, and so do Becky and Chad and Mr. Carlson, all of whom want Mrs. Tweezes and Milton to stay. The parrot is asking for justice. He, too, says that fairness is important.

7. When Mr. Carlson and Mrs. Tweezes and the children talk about the problem they decide to go and see Mr.

Bradley. They decide that this might be the best way to solve the problem. Why do they do this? They are saying that talking things over is important, and they are also saying that this is a good way to solve a problem.

Value identification in folktale

"The Princess and the Pomegranate" is a Jewish folktale. It is a variation of the story of winning the princess which appears in many cultures. An additional element in this tale, which is a theme common to many Jewish folktales, is the solving of a riddle or rendering of judgement. In this case the judgment involves a moral value: The greatest gifts are those that cost the giver something. Or, an alternate interpretation, to deserve the love of others one must give of oneself.

"The Princess and the Pomegranate"

Once upon a time there were three brothers. Their father told them as he was dying that they should take the money that he had saved and travel into the world. He said that each one would find a special gift and together they would gain a kingdom.

When their father died the brothers followed his instructiions and set off into the world, looking for the special gifts. They had not gone far when they came to the seacoast, and there the brothers met an old sailor. "Please," said the sailor, "I need some money. I will sell you this spyglass for whatever money you have. It is a very special spyglass; it can see everywhere in the world."

"That is indeed a special gift," said the eldest brother, and he gave the sailor all his money for the spyglass. And the brothers continued on their was. Next they come to a desert, and sitting under the shade of a rocky cliff, they met a man with a rolled up carpet. The brothers shared their food and drink with the man. Ather their meal the man said to them, "I would like to reward you for your kindness. I will sell you this carpet for whatever money you have. It is a very special carpet, for all you need to do is sit upon it and command it to take you wherever you want to go."

"This must be my gift," said the second brother. And he gave the merchant all his silver for the carpet. Next they came to a forest and as they traveled through it they come to a tree of glowing beauty and bright color. They stopped to admire it, but could find no fruit. Then the youngest brother saw on a branch, just above his head, a single pomegranate, looking like a red moon. "This must be my gift," he said and plucked the pomegranate from the tree. No sooner had he done so than another pomegranate appeared in its place.

"This is indeed a special pomegranate," said the youngest brother.

"But what does it do?" asked the others. "You have not chosen well," they said.

"Never mind," said the youngest, "I will know what to do when the time comes."

The eldest brother said, "We shall see. I don't think a pomegranate can help us no matter how beautiful it is . But we shall see."

And he picked up his spyglass and began to look as far as he could, all over the world. He stopped when he saw a king in deep grief. He was sitting by the bedside of a beautiful princess. As he told his brothers what he saw, the second brother unrolled the carpet. The three brothers sat upon it and it flew to that faraway kingdom.

As they arrived, the king announced that whoever could cure the princess would marry her and inherit the kingdom. The youngest brother approached the king. "I can cure the princess," he said. And when he was shown into the princess' room, the youngest brother took out the pomegranate and broke it open. With every seed he fed the princess she grew stronger.

At last she arose from her bed in perfect health.

The kingdom rejoiced, but when it came time to announce the wedding each of the brothers claimed the princess.

The eldest brother said, "Without me and my special spyglass, you would not ever have seen or known about the princess."

The second brother said, "True, but without my special carpet, we could not have come to the kingdom and the princess would still be ill."

The king listened to these arguments and was puzzled. All three brothers together had cured the princess. He looked at the princess who was much known for her wisdom. "Can you show us the truth?" he asked. "Whose claim is not just?"

The princess smiled. She turned to the eldest brother. Do you still have your special spyglass?" she asked.

"Yes," he said, "here it is."

The princess turned to the second brother. "Do you still have your special carpet?" she asked.

"Yes," he said, "here it is."

The princess turned to the youngest brother. "Do you still have your special pomegranate?" she asked.

The youngest brother shook his head sadly, "No," he said.

But the princess smiled. "There is the answer," she said. "Only you have given away your gift in curing me. Therefore you have done the most and your claim is most just."

And the princess took his hand, and everyone acknowledged that the princess was as wise as she was beautiful. So they were married and ruled in peace for many years.

Teaching Strategies

After the teacher has read to the class, the story of "The Princess and the Pomegranate", ask the class "What is the best kind of gift to give someone?" While reading the story, stop before the princess makes her decision and ask the class "Which brother did the most to cure the princess and why do you think so?" (Read the rest of the story and compare the princess' answer to the student's answers.

Other questions for discussion are:

1. How did each brother contribute to curing the princess?
2. Do you agree with the judgment of the Princess? Do you agree with her reason?
3. Do you know any other stories or folktales in which a magic gift is given? What was the gift? What happened as a result?
4. What values does the Princess' judgment illustrate?

Assign the students to read and retell or write a folktale from another culture that has the theme of the giving of a gift.

Selected Literature on Values

Primary Grades

Neslon, Vaunda M. *Always Grandma*. New York: Putnam 1988
Steptoe, John. *Mufaro's Beautiful Daughters: An African Tale*. Lothrop, 1987
Steptoe, John, *Stevie*. Harper, 1969
Steig, William. *Brave Irene*

Intermediate Grades

Paterson, Katherine. *The Great Billy Hopkins*. New York: Crowell, 1978.

Groves, Vicki. *Good-bye, My Wishing Star*. New York: Putnam, 1988

Talbert, Marc. *Toby*. Dial, 1987.

Upper Grades

Hamilton, Virginia. Anthony Burns: *The Defeat and Triumph of a Fugitive Slave*. New York: Knopf, 1988.

Self-Concept: Bibliography

Baecher, R. E., et al. (1989). <u>Preventive Strategies and Effective Practices for At-Risk Children in Urban Elementary Schools</u>. Paper presented at the Annual Meeting of the American Educational Research Association, San Francisco.

Barnes, B., Mason, E., Leary, M. R., Laurent, J., et al. (1988). Reactions to Social vs. Self-Evaluation: Moderating Effects of Personal and Social Identity Orientations. <u>Journal of Research in Personality</u>, 22, 4 513-524.

Beane, J.A., Lipka, R.P. (1986). <u>Self-Concept, Self-Esteem and the Curriculum</u>, Teacher's College Press: New York.

Brown, J. D.; Collins, R. & Schmidt, G. W. (1988). Self-esteem and direct vs. indirect forms of self-enhancement. <u>Journal of Personality and Social Psychology</u> 55, 3, 445-453.

Burke, J. P., et al (1985). The Role of Self-Esteem in Affective Reactions to Achievement-Related Situations. <u>Educational and Psychological Research</u>, 5, 191-203.

Careaga, R. Comp. National Clearinghouse for Bilingual Education, Wheaton, Md., Office of Bilingual Education and Minority Languages Affairs (Ed), Washington, D.C.

Combs, C. (1964). Perception of Self and Scholastic Underachievement in the Academically Capable. <u>Personnel and Guidance</u>. 42, 42-51.

Coopersmith, S. (1968). Studies in Self-Esteem. <u>Scientific American</u>, 218, 96-102.

Dresden, J., Meyers, B.K. (1989). <u>Young Children</u>, 44, 62-66. Early Childhood Professionals: Toward Self-Definition.

Faust, V. (1980). <u>Self-Esteem in the Classroom</u>. San Diego: Thomas Paine Press.

Fink, M.B. (1962). Self-concept as it's Related to Academic Under Achievement. <u>California Journal of Educational Research</u>, 13, 57-62.

Greenberg, P. (1989). "Ideas that Work with Young Children Learning Self-Esteem and Self-Discipline through Play." <u>Young Children</u>, 44, 28-31.

Greene, B. & Uroff, S. (1989). Achievement through Self-Esteem. <u>Educational Leadership</u>, Apollo High School, 46, 5, 80-81.

Greenwald, A. G. & Bellezza, F. S., Banajl A., Mahzarin R. (1988). Is Self-Esteem a Central Ingredient of the Self-Concept? <u>Personality and Social Psychology Bulletin</u>, 14, 1, 34-45.

Hardeman, Carole Hall. (1985). The Quest for Excellence/Pupil Self-Esteem. National Center for Education Statistics, in Invited Papers Elementary/Secondary Education Data Redesign Project: Washington, D.C.

Hollins, E.R. (1982). The Marva Collins Story Revisited: Implications for Regular Classroom Instruction. <u>Journal of Teacher Education</u>, 33, 1, 37-40.

Holly, W.J. (1987). Students' Self-Esteem and Academic Achievement. National Association of Elementary School Principals: Virginia, 4, 1.

Khan, Sar B., Alvi, Sabir A. (1983). Educational, social and psychological correlates of vocational maturity. <u>Journal of Vocational Behavior</u>, 22, 3, 357-364.

Kostelnik, M.J. (1988). Children's Self-Esteem: The Verbal Environment. <u>Childhood Education</u>, 65, 29-32.

Lillemyr, O. F. (1982). The Relationship of Self-Perceptions and Achievement Motives in Norwegian Children. Paper presented at the Annual Meeting of the American Educational Research Association, 66th:New York.

Lyman, L., Foyle, H.C. (1984). Comparative Learning in the Middle School. Paper presented at the Annual Kansas Symposium for Middle Level Education, 12th:Kansas.

Milner, Russel. (1987). Self-esteem and role-taking ability. Journal of Child Care. 3, 3, 9-15.

Schneider, M. J., Leitenberg, H. (1989). A comparison of aggressive and withdrawn children's self-esteem, optimism and pessimism, and causal attributions for success and failure. Journal of Abnormal Child Psychology, 17, 2, 133-144.

Street, S. (1988). "Feedback and Self-Concept in High School Students." Adolescence, 23, 449-456.

Tunney, J. (1984). Self-Esteem and Participation: 2 Basics for Student Achievement. NASSP Bulletin, 68, 117-21.

Walker, L.S.; Greene, J.W. (1986). "The Social Context of Adolescent Self-Esteem," Journal of Youth & Adolescence, 15, 4.

Waterman, A.S. (1985). Identity in the context of adolescent psychology. New Directions for Child Development, Trenton State College:N.J., 30, 5, 24.

Yawkey, Thomas D. (1980). The Self-Concept of the Young Child. Brigham Young University Press:Utah.

Zuckerman, D.M. (1985). Confidence and Aspirations: Self-esteem and self-concepts as predictors of students' life goals. Journal of Personality, 53, 4, 543-560.

Values: Bibliography

Bandura, A. & MacDonald, F. (1963). "Influence of Social Reinforcement and the Behavior Models in Shaping Children's Moral Judgment" Journal of Abnormal and Social Psychology 67, 3, 274-81.

Boehm, L. (1962). "Development of Conscience: A Comparison of American Children of Different Mental and Socio-Economic Levels" Child Development, 33, 575-90.

Brodbeck, A.J. (1954). "Learning Theory and Identification: Motivation as a Determinant of Conscience Development." Journal of Genetic Psychology, 84, 219-227.

Bauer, G.L. (1987). Teaching morality in the classroom. Education Digest, 52, 2, 4.

Comer J.P. (1989). Teaching your kids values. (11- through 13-year-olds). Parents Magazine, 64, 220, 1.

DeCaspner, H.S. & Tittle, C.K. (1988). Rankings and ratings of values: Counseling uses suggested by factoring two types of scales for female and male eleventh grade students. Educational & Psychological Measurement, 48, 2, 375-384.

Errington, P.I. (1982). A Question of Values Iowa State U Press, 196.

Gallagher, A.F. (1988). In Search of Justice: The Thousand-Mile Walkathon. Social-Education, 52, 7, 527-31.

Goldbecker, S.S. (1976). Values Teaching. National Education Association: Washington.

Gordon, T. T.E.T. (Teacher Effectiveness Training). Wyden Publising: New York.
Harmin, M. (1977). What I've Learned about Values Education. Phil Delta Kappa.

Havighurst, R.J., Robinson, P.J., & Dorr, M. (1946). "The Development of the Ideal Self in Childhood and Adolescence" <u>Journal of Educational Research</u>, 4, 241-257.

Hendricks, W. (1984). Values suggested activities to motivate the teaching of values. Ed Service:Michigan.

Hester, J.P. & Killian, D.R. (1984). <u>Cartoons for Thinking</u>: <u>Issues in Ethics & Values</u>. Trillium Press, 198.

Hodge, R.L. (1989). A Myriad of Values: A Brief History. Paper presented at the Annual Conference of the American Educational Research Association, 70th, California.

Salk, L. (1988). How to teach your child values. 115, 43, 1.

Vasquez, J.A., et al. (1983). <u>Values & Minorities: An Annotated Bibliography</u>. National Clearinghouse Bilingual Educational: Wheaton.

Problem Solving: Bibliography

Bingham, A. (1988). _Improving Children's Facility in Problem Solving_. Bureau of Publications: New York.

Hartup, W.W., et al. (1988). Conflict and the Friendship Relations of Young Children. _Child Development_, 59, 6.

Hollaway, O. (1975). _Problem Solving: Toward a More Humanizing Curriculum_. Franklin Publishing: Philadelphia.

Laughter, K.G. (1988). Nothing Was Ever Timothy's Fault. _Learning_, 16, 9, 38-40.

Laursen, B., Hartup, W.W. (1989). The Dynamics of Preschool Children's Conflicts. Merrill-Palmer-Quarterly, 35, 3, 281-97.

Lechner, M. (1988). The Process of Consensus. _Experiential Education_, 11, 3, 10-14.

Passe, J. (1988). Developing Current Events Awareness in Children. _Social Education_, 52, 7 531-33.

Peirce, K., Edwards, E.D. (1988). Children's Construction of Fantasy Stories: Gender Differences in Conflict Resolution Strategies. _Sex-Roles_, 18, 7-8, 393-404.

Pezdek, K. (1987). _Applications of Cognitive Psychology: Problem Solving, Education, and Computing_. L. Erlbaum Associates: New Jersey.

Rich, J.M. (1972). _Conflict and Decision. Analyzing Educational Issues_. Harper and Row: New York.

Stievater, S.M. (1985). Bibliography of recent doctoral dissertations on creativity and problem solving. _Journal of Creative Behavior_, 19, 4, 283-294.

Welch, G. (1989). How We Keep Our Playground from Becoming a Battlefield. _Executive Educator_, 11, 5, 23-31.